MARITIME
GREENWICH

MARITIME
GREENWICH

DAVID
RAMZAN

FRONTISPIECE: Greenwich Hospital and the hospital ship
Dreadnaught moored off Deptford Creek. From a print of a
lithograph by W. Parrott, *c.*1840.

First published 2009
Reprinted, 2019

The History Press
97 St George's Place
Gloucestershire, GL50 3QB
www.thehistorypress.co.uk

© David Ramzan, 2009

The right of David Ramzan to be identified as the Author
of this work has been asserted in accordance with the
Copyrights, Designs and Patents Act 1988.

All rights reserved. No part of this book may be reprinted
or reproduced or utilised in any form or by any electronic,
mechanical or other means, now known or hereafter invented,
including photocopying and recording, or in any information
storage or retrieval system, without the permission in writing
from the Publishers.
British Library Cataloguing in Publication Data.
A catalogue record for this book is available from the British Library.

ISBN 978 07524 4778 0

Typesetting and origination by The History Press
Printed in Great Britain by TJ International Lrd, Padstow, Cornwall.

CONTENTS

ACKNOWLEDGEMENTS

The images contained in this publication are from my personal collection and from the Local History Library at the Greenwich Heritage Centre. I should like to thank the staff at the library who were always more than helpful in supplying images and invaluable information to help me in compiling this publication. I should like to thank my own family and friends, whom over the years have provided information of their own time living and working in the area, and recalling local stories and information passed down to them from an even older generation. I should also like to thank all those who have provided specific historical information, including the Port of London Authority, the Museum in Docklands, the Greenwich Industrial Heritage Society, the National Maritime Museum and the Cutty Sark Trust. If for any reason I have not accredited any images to people or organisations as necessary, or failed to trace any copyright holders, then I should like to apologise for any oversight.

Photographic credits: The Greenwich Heritage Centre, A. Phinbow, and D. Ramzan.

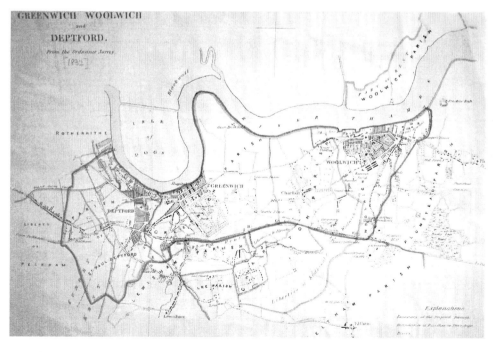

Map of Greenwich, Woolwich and Deptford c.1832. Three areas where London's role in shipbuilding began.

INTRODUCTION

The River Thames at the turn of the twenty-first century, a vast expanse of water with not a single ship to be seen. At one time the riverfront would be filled with cranes, wharfs and ships loading or un-loading their cargos. A multitude of river craft from small rowboats to giant steamers would have once been seen making their way along this point in the river. Times have changed and the Thames at Greenwich is no longer the busy waterways it once was.

Anyone standing on the south bank of the river Thames at Greenwich Reach will look out upon an area of regeneration and change. As the Thames winds its way downriver you can look in any direction at this point and will see this once-busy commercial river now devoid of the ships, wharves and warehousing that once filled this stretch of waterway.

The occasional tug may be seen towing barges along the river, and one or two of the few remaining working vessels still operating on the Thames may pass you by, but it is more likely the craft you will see are pleasure boats taking tourists back and forth from Greenwich Pier to the Tower of London, or one of the new, fast, sleek passenger ferries transporting commuters upriver to their place of work and back again. Most of the wharfs and warehouses that once stood on the frontage of the capital city's river are gone, replaced by hotels, restaurants and luxury apartments. The street names are the only clue left to remind you of the area's great seafaring heritage.

Being born in Greenwich, I lived and played as a youngster close to the river Thames, from a time when ships from all parts of the world would tie up at the wharves and warehouses lining my local stretch of the river. Merchant seamen from all corners of the globe, speaking many different languages, would frequent the many inns and public houses found nestling between riverside buildings or standing on the corners of streets made up of rows and rows of two-up, two-down terraced housing. The wharves, ships and barges were our adventure playground, and there were many occasions when my friends and I were chased off by the Thames River Police who patrolled the river. The area has seen continued change and evolution during the past fifty years of my own life, with the once-busy metropolis of shipping now gone, along with much of the area's rich history and heritage.

Of course, the famous Greenwich landmarks still remain, such as the old Royal Naval College (now the University of Greenwich), and the National Maritime Museum, once a school for boy sailors, but many of the places from the shipping and maritime days have been demolished to make way for hotels, residential properties and leisure facilities. Many of the old commercial buildings that remain have been converted into modern luxury flats and apartments.

The area has recently seen many new innovative developments, such as the Dome on the Greenwich Peninsular, the Thames Barrier near Woolwich and the London Docklands Light Railway running from south of the river to the north, all marvels of modern technology and engineering. At one time it was the ships, shipbuilding and shipping that was synonymous with new technology and engineering throughout the boroughs of Greenwich, Deptford and Woolwich. The only ship found in the area today is the landlocked clipper *Cutty Sark*, undergoing complete renovation herself, very close to where great warships were once built ,and merchant ships of wood and iron were launched into the waters of the River Thames.

For over a thousand years this part of the river was the site of a thriving ship and boat-building industry, from small Peter boats that fished the upper and lower stretches of the Thames, to great oak-built vessels of war that sailed the seas and oceans across the globe.

After the Romans landed in Britain some 2,000 years ago, London became a major shipping port and, later, a centre for shipbuilding. A variety of ships were built up and down the Thames, but it was on the south bank of the river where London's shipbuilding evolved, when the Royal Docks of Deptford and Woolwich were established by King Henry VIII, whose palace stood between the two at Greenwich. On Greenwich Peninsular, Greenwich Marsh, all types of river craft and seagoing vessels were once built, and the marsh area would gradually become a vast commercial zone for the manufacture of all types of shipping and industrial commodities.

Throughout this publication I have collected a series of images to reflect the area's wonderful, lost maritime heritage, from the ships and the shipbuilding industries to the people and places of times past. Although this publication is not a definitive history of Maritime Greenwich, as it would take volumes to give the subject the justice it deserves, I hope that I have shown enough within these pages to give readers an insight into a maritime heritage now long gone, a heritage that is sadly and gradually fading into history.

D. Ramzan
December 2008

One

Royal Docks

During the reign of Henry VII the first royal dockyard was established at Portsmouth on the South Coast of England. Great wooden ships were to be built there, to export goods to ports throughout the Continent and to be used as vessels of war. Most vessels during this period were merchant ships, with men and armaments, small canon, bows and arrows taken on board as required, when ships were needed in times of war.

When Henry VIII came to the thrown his priority was to construct a fleet of warships the like that no seafaring nation had seen before. Portsmouth was a long journey from London for a king who wanted to oversee the development of his navy, so two royal dockyards were established at Deptford and Woolwich, both being a short horse, carriage or boat ride away from the King's royal palace at Greenwich.

The areas of Deptford and Woolwich grew with the development of the Royal Docks, creating jobs and employment for hundreds of sailors, shipwrights, carpenters, rope makers and sail makers. Later, armaments manufacturing would be carried out close to the docks in Woolwich when the Royal Arsenal was established in the late 1600s, and during the 1700s a large victualling yard was built next to the docks in Deptford to store ships' goods and provisions, making this area of south London the most important in Britain's maritime history.

An engraving from the early seventeenth century, showing Deptford Royal Docks towards the left of the illustration, as viewed from Greenwich. From here, Henry VIII would have been able to watch his ships being built from his palace overlooking the Thames.

Above: A view of the Royal Docks at Deptford during the late 1600s. Before the Royal Docks were established, Deptford was already an important centre for trade with locally built ships journeying to Europe and beyond during the early Tudor period.

Right: List of Elder Brethren of the Corporation of Trinity House published in the early 1600s, including notable diarist Samuel Pepys. Pepys was best known for his written eyewitness accounts of London's great plague and fire. Attached to the Navy in many official rolls during his life, he was once imprisoned in the Tower of London as a spy on accusations of selling naval information to the French, a charge later dropped for lack of evidence.

A List of the Thirty One **ELDER-BRETHREN** *appointed by the* **CHARTER** *of King* **JAMES** *the Second.*

Master,
SAMUEL PEPYS, *Esq;*
Wardens.

Capt. John Nicholls | *Cap.* Nicholas Kerington
Capt. Henry Mudd | *Capt.* William Green

Assistants,

Henry *Duke of* Grafton | *Sir* Thomas Allen, *Kt. and Baronet.*
William *Earl of* Craven | *Capt.* Simon Nicholls
George *Earl of* Berkely | *Capt.* Isaac Woodgreen
George *Lord* Dartmouth | *Capt.* Thomas Browne.

Elder Brethren,

Sir Rich. Haddock, *Kt.* | *Capt.* Anthony Young
Sir John Berry, *Kt.* | *Capt.* John Hill
Sir John Narbrough, *Kt* | *Capt.* Francis Wilshaw
Sir Matth. Andrews, *Kt.* | *Capt.* Robert Fisher
Sir Anthony Dean, *Kt.* | *Capt.* James Bonnell
Capt. Henry Sheere | *Capt.* Ralph Sanderson
Capt. Hugh Till | *Capt.* Thomas Wilshaw
Capt. Samuel Chamblet | *Capt.* Samuel Rutter
Capt. Thomas Collier | *Capt.* Richard Goodlad

THE ROYAL

CHARTER

OF

CONFIRMATION

GRANTED BY

His most excellent MAJESTY

King JAMES II.

TO THE

TRINITY-HOUSE

OF

Deptford-Strond ;

For the Government and Increase of the

NAVIGATION OF ENGLAND,

And the Relief of Poor

Mariners, their Widows, and Orphans, &c.

LONDON: Printed in the Year 1763.

The cover of a Royal Charter for Trinity House at Deptford granted by the King, *c.*1763. Henry VIII established Trinity House in 1514 at Deptford Strand, which worked as an association of mariners and shipmen in support of English naval and merchant shipping, providing navigational aids, lighthouses, light vessels and buoys. Trinity House also provided accommodation for former naval personnel and seamen.

Opposite above: Elizabeth I knights Sir Francis Drake on the *Golden Hind* at Deptford on 4 April 1581. When Drake's ship later became redundant she was laid up at Deptford Creek, close to the dockyard, as a memorial to his exploits on behalf of England and the Crown. There she remained for many years, until falling into decay and eventually being broken up. All that remains of this historic ship is a chair made from her timbers presented to the University of Oxford.

Opposite below: Ships moored off Deptford Dockyard, *c.*1700, with Greenwich Hospital in the distance. Naval vessels were not the only craft operating from these dockyards – trading ships sailed out of Deptford importing and exporting goods from all corners of the world, including human cargo. For more than 200 years the dockyards in Deptford were used as a port by captains and merchants who profited from the slave trade up until abolition in 1807.

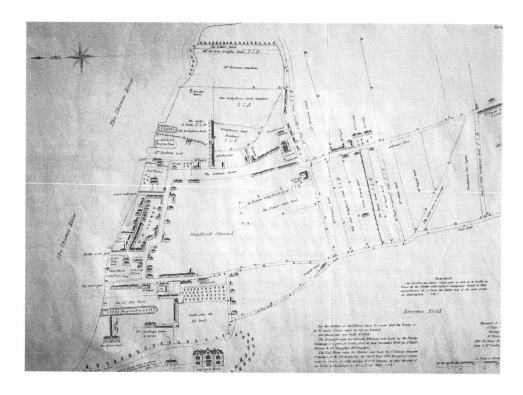

Above: Map of Deptford, *c.*1623, with additions by John Evelyn showing the docks, houses, street plans and land owned by the King. John Evelyn was a prolific author and published books on architecture, theology, horticulture and politics. He settled with his wife in a house, Sayes Court, purchased from his father-in-law, Sir Richard Browne, which can be seen located at the base of the map next to the Royal Dockyard.

Left: Peter Czar of Muscovy, or Peter the Great as he became known, inspecting a ship being built in Deptford Dockyard during his four-month stay in 1698. He came to Deptford to study the latest developments in shipbuilding, and resided near the Royal Dockyard at the home of John Evelyn during his stay.

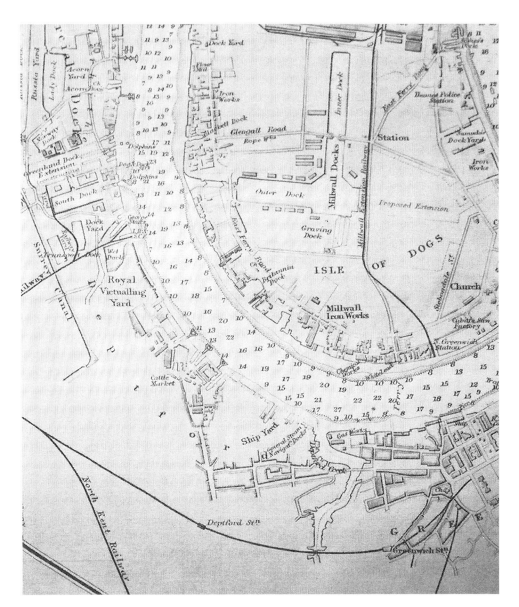

A print of a map of Deptford from the 1800s showing the site, described then as a cattle market and shipyard, of the Royal Docks after closure in 1869. In the middle of the map can be seen the victualling yards and, higher up, the commercial docks that eventually became the most important area for commercial shipping on the south side of the Thames.

The mouth of Deptford Creek, from an engraving, *c.*1810. The creek divided Deptford from Greenwich and at one time the only crossing between the two was by way of Deptford Bridge on the river Ravensbourne. The creek is the tidal mouth of this small river that flows into the Thames by Greenwich Reach. After the Royal Docks closed, private shipping and commercial industries built up on both side of this waterway.

An early 1800s etching of Trinity Hospital, showing the frontage of the building that was erected in 1672 in Church Street, Deptford, on land donated by Sir Richard Browne. The almshouses, built close to the Royal Docks, were specifically for the sailors who had once served their country, and were retired, in ill health or suffering an injury. The hospital was demolished in 1877.

Above: Henry VIII Storehouse at Deptford Royal Docks depicted during the early 1800s. Henry VIII revolutionised shipbuilding during his reign and built great storehouses within the dockyard to contain all the supplies required for shipbuilding, and to equip the ships sailing from their berths at Deptford.

Right: An original window from the storehouse discovered after bomb damage to buildings in the Deptford Dockyard area during the Second World War. After the Royal Docks closed in 1869 many of the buildings were reused as storehouses, included within later building developments or demolished completely after bomb damage during the Second World War.

School House on Deptford Green.   Admiral Hughes's House Deptford.

School at Deptford Green and Admiral Hughes' house dipicted in a drawing from the early 1800s. Deptford Green bordered the south of the Royal Docks with houses, schools, shops and inns built close by to accomdate the ever-increasing population moving into Deptford to work at the dockyards. There is still a Deptford Green School close to the original site of the dockyards, but almost all of the original period properties from that time have long gone.

Chimney Piece in the Admiralty Board Room. Gun Tavern Deptford.

An illustration from the early seventeenth century, depicting the chimneypiece in the Admiralty Board Room at the Gun Tavern, once the house of the Earl of Nottingham, Lord High Admiral of England, who played a large part in the defeat of the Spanish Armada. It was his armorial bearings that were carved over the chimneypiece, and were proudly shown to visitors by the Admiralty in Deptford Dockyard.

Above: East India tradesman in Deptford dock, *c.*1824. The East India Company were granted an English Royal Charter by Elizabeth I in 1600. The Royal Charter effectively gave the company a monopoly on all trade in the East Indies. Ships owned by the East India Company were built in yards leased at Deptford until the seventeenth century, when costs dictated that it would be more financially beneficial to lease ships rather than build them.

Right: St Nicholas Church today, one of the remaining building from the time the docks were in use during the sixteenth century. Admiral Hughes was Commissioner of the Navy during the late 1700s and his memorial can be found in the church. St Nicholas was the patron saint of sailors and on the gate piers at the entrance to the church grounds are a pair of skulls with crossbones, a symbol that was used by pirates on their ships' flags.

Deptford Royal Dockyard depicted during the late sixteenth century. In the distance can be seen the Royal Palace of Placentia at Greenwich, birthplace of Henry VIII and his daughters, Mary and Elizabeth. When Henry VIII became King in 1509, there were only five royal warships; by the time of his death in 1547, the Navy had a complement of around forty.

The old and the new, the original gates to the Royal Victoria Victualling Yards from 1858 with the recently re-furbished Aragon Tower, once part of Pepys Estate, in the background. The majority of the houses and flats that covered the old Royal Dockyard site were predominantly built for council tenants, but are now once again in the process of complete regeneration.

The launch of the 26-gun, 4,538-ton screw frigate *Ariadne* at Deptford in 1859, ten years prior to the dockyard's closure. After the Napoleonic Wars naval shipbuilding went into decline, and with the dockyard unable to expand due to the increase in the development of commercial and private property bordering the yards, the days of building great men-of-war finally came to an end. The dockyard became a cattle market that operated until 1931, and was then gradually redeveloped into housing and industrial buildings after much of the area was bombed during the Second World War.

A contemporary monument to Peter the Great at Millennium Quay on the Deptford side of the Creek, unveiled by Prince Michael of Kent in 2001. The Czar was instrumental in taking western technologies and designs into Russia, so would probably feel at home standing in front of this development of modern apartments.

Woolwich Royal Dockyard, c.1788. Woolwich had once been used as a port by the Anglo-Saxons for the exporting and trading of wool, but was no more than a small riverside village before the Royal Dockyard was established in 1512. In the illustration several large warships are on the slips, either in for repair, refitting or under construction.

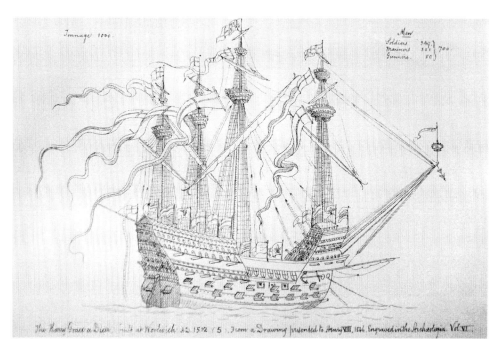

An illustration of the most famous ship built at Woolwich, *Henri Grace De Dieu,* better known as the *Great Harry.* Henry VIII wanted the biggest and best ship ever to have sailed the seas, and in 1512 commissioned the building of this huge vessel. Completed in 1514, she carried a complement of 700 men, made up of mariners, soldiers and gunners. The drawing was made specifically for Henry VIII, and presented to him in 1546, a year before his death.

A fully rigged ship and another, possibly waiting to be fitted out, moored off Woolwich Dockyard in the mid-1700s. Since Tudor times the British Navy had been in conflict with the navies of both Spain and France, and Woolwich had become a major seafaring industrial area for both war and trade.

A model showing the stern of the first-rate ship of the line, *Sovereign of the Seas*, launched at Woolwich in 1637. The ship, designed and built by Peter Pett, son of the master shipwright to Charles I, was the most extravagantly decorated warship in the Royal Navy. The building costs of just over £65,000 caused a financial crisis for the Crown, contributing towards the outbreak of the Civil War. In regular service for more than fifty years, the *Sovereign of the Seas* saw action in the first Anglo-Dutch war, and the War of the Grand Alliance against Louise XIV of France. While laid up at Chatham in January 1696, the ship was burned down to the waterline in mysterious circumstances.

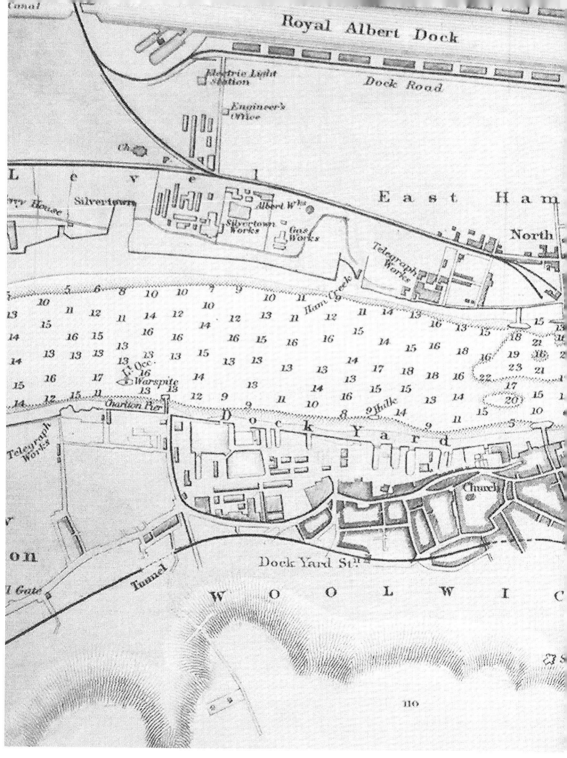

A map of Woolwich from the late 1800s, showing the Royal Dockyard to the left and Royal Arsenal to the right. By the mid-1800s, there was the need for much bigger ships than the dockyard could produce, and with the Thames silting up causing problems in launching ships with a deep draft, the dockyards eventually closed down in 1869.

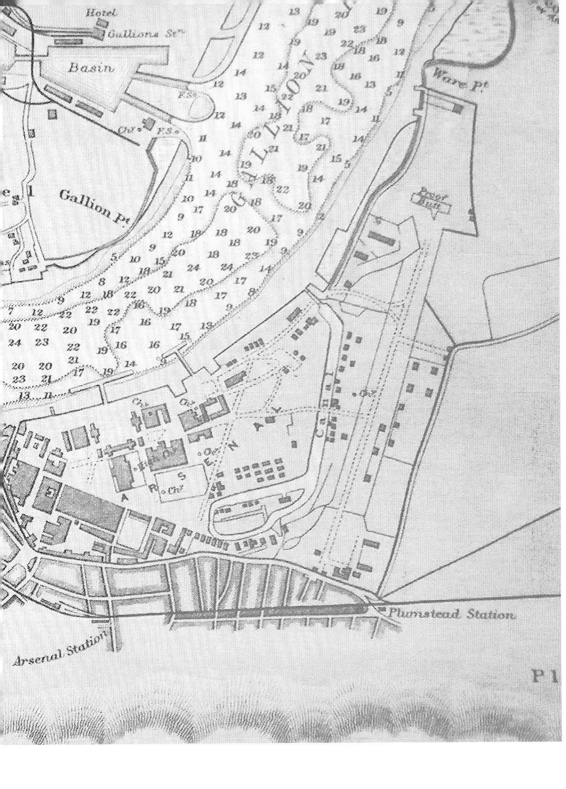

Convicts at work at Woolwich Dockyard during the 1700s. Many convicts, either sentenced or awaiting sentence, carried out hard labour on the docks, from moving stores and hardware to carrying out ground works and repairs required in the dockyards. Many of these convicts found themselves transported to the colonies on ships sailing from the Woolwich Dockyard.

Convict hulk *Unite* moored off Woolwich Dockyard during the mid-1800s. After the transportation of convicts to the Americas ceased in 1776, convicts were kept on board old warships while working on the dockyards. However, prisoners were still being transported to Australia, and many could spend years on these ships living in terrible conditions while awaiting passage.

Convicts working on the foreshore at Woolwich during the 1700s. Both the Royal Dockyards of Deptford and Woolwich used almost 1,000 convicts a day for manual labour. Those unfortunates that died while working at the docks or on board the hulks at Woolwich were thrown into the marshes near the dockyards. Some years later, a large quantity of bones were unearthed when building work was being carried out at the new Arsenal factories. Using hulks for the accommodation of convicts ended in 1856.

Anchor chains being tested at Woolwich Dockyard in the early 1800s. A majority of the residents of Woolwich worked in the dockyards and adjacent armaments site at the Royal Arsenal.

One of the Woolwich workers from the metal factory established in the dockyard during the 1800s. Many other industries built up within the dockyard and surrounding area included metal-working factories making anchors and chains, gun bastions, ropeyards and steam-engine factories.

Anchor-testing workshop at Woolwich Dockyard during the late 1800s. In 1809 the Royal Navy established a scale that specified the correct type and number of anchors required for various classes of ship. Some of the largest anchors ever made came out of the Woolwich foundry during this time.

Launch of the Nelson at Woolwich. July 4th 1814. from a Drawing by Clennell.

A ship named after a famous British Admiral, *Nelson* is launched at Woolwich in 1814. A first-rate ship of the line, HMS *Nelson* weighed 2,617 tons, carried 120 guns and had a complement of more than 800 men. In 1869 she was fitted out with a steam engine and screw for extra propulsion. At the end of her service, in 1928, the ship was broken up.

HMS *Boscawen*, launched at Woolwich in 1844, was a three-decked sailing ship of the line. During the Russian War *Boscawen* was patrolling the Baltic Sea, and on 15 April 1854 she captured the Russian brig *Patrioten*. At the end of her sailing days, in 1862, she became a training vessel for young sailors at Portland.

HMS *Thunderer* at her launch at Woolwich in 1831. This 84-gun second-rate battleship looked much like others of her class, but she was built using a new design feature where the ship's wooden ribs would be interlaced diagonally, and the hull and deck planking fitted in alternating diagonal layers, giving the ship greater strength.

Celebrations at the *Thunderer's* launch at Woolwich in 1831. Nine years after her launch the ship took part in the Battle of Sidon, the last action where the British Navy used wooden-built battleships under sail. During the same year, the *Thunderer* also acted as flagship for the bombardment and capture of the fortress at St Jean d'Acre, where steam-powered warships saw action for the first time as support vessels. The ship remained in service for another thirty years.

First-rate ship of the line *Trafalgar* on the slips at Woolwich in 1841. From the time of Henry VIII, British warships were built using oak grown on these shores. To build a 500-ton ship you would need enough oak to cover 12 acres of land – approximately eighty years of growth – so it was no surprise that oak started to become a very rare commodity in the building of ships.

HMS *Trafalgar* is launched at Woolwich in June 1841. These ship launches became a huge spectacle for the workers at the dockyards and people from the local area. On the river, ships and boats would be crammed with onlookers trying to get a view of these huge men-of-war sliding majestically into the water.

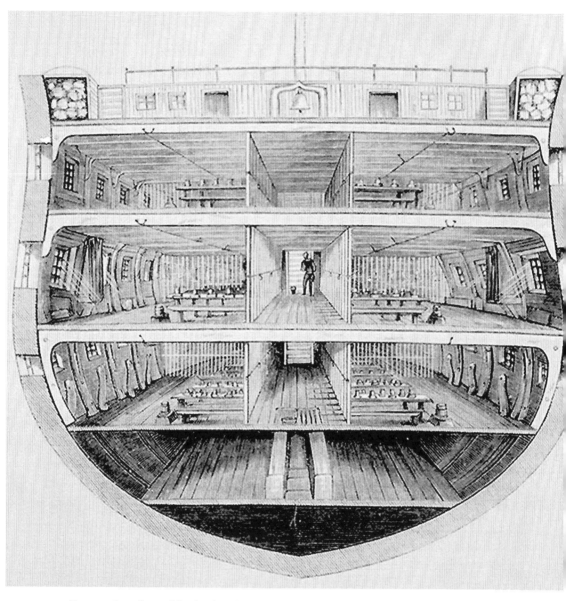

Cross-section of one of the first broadside, iron-clad warships built after the famous HMS *Warrior* and *Black Prince*. From the the second half of the nineteenth century, iron-clad warships were replacing wooden ships. The Admiralty was requesting a class of larger warship that carried the same armour as the *Warrior*, but that was more economic to build than the first two iron clads, although Lord Palmerstone, the Prime Minister at the time, was not convinced that wooden-built warships had seen their day. Consequently, Woolwich was required to build iron as well as wooden ships.

The first Royal Navy screw frigate to be built, *Amphion*, launched at Woolwich in 1846. The wooden-built ship had been intended as sail only, but was converted on the stocks into a steam-powered, screw-propelled vessel. With engines attaining 300hp, the frigate could reach speeds of just over 5 knots. The ship's propeller measured 14ft in diameter, and it was stated at the time that the ship's performance proved so successful that the use of screw propellers would become universal for war steamers in the future. The ship was paid off and sold for breaking in 1863.

HMS *Spitfire*, a wooden-built paddle steamer, before her launch at Woolwich in 1845. The gun vessel operated in the Mediterranean and Black Sea during the Russian War. There had been several ships in the Royal Navy to carry the name *Spitfire*, all named after a Spanish treasure gallion captured by Sir Francis Drake.

War paddle steamer the *Terrible* in a basin at Woolwich Dockyard a year after her launch there in 1845. The Navy had been considering the use of iron in warship construction since Brunel had built the *Great Britain* in 1843, and following experimentation in the design and building of iron paddle steamers this was carried out when the Navy commisioned a larger type of iron paddle frigate to be built. The *Terrible* was one of these new type of frigates, and fought in the Crimean War. Problems encountered with paddle steamers during warfare, mainly due to the large paddle wheels sustaining damage under fire, led to their demise in favour of screw propeller-built warships.

Fifity-gun, fourth-rate ship of the line *Nankin*, launched at Woolwich in March 1850. HMS *Nankin* served in the East Indies, and was involved in several actions carried out in the Second Anglo-Chinese War.

In May 1853, the battleship HMS *Agamemnon* was launched at Woolwich Dockyard, the first warship to be built keel upwards to include a steam engine. Steam power at this period was relatively poor for ships the size of the *Agamemnon*, so she was designed to carry a full square rig on three masts. During 1857 and 1858 she was equipped to carry telegraph cable, attempting to lay the eastern half of the transatlantic cable to Newfoundland from Ireland.

Cannon shot being unloaded at the Warren Woolwich Dockyard in 1855. The Warren was the depot for ordnance belonging to the Royal Navy. On the site was a foundry for making canons, a laboratory and a repository for military hardware for use on sea and land. All ordnance made by contractors outside of the docks had to be tested on the site before approval was given for its use on naval ships.

Queen Victoria launches the *Royal Albert*, the ship named in honour of her husband, the Prince Consort, in May 1854. Over 200ft in length, the ship carried 121 guns and a complement of over 1,000 men.

Leaving the slips on her launch in 1854, the *Royal Albert* slides into the Thames at Woolwich. A wooden-built ship powered by sail and steam engine, the *Royal Albert* suffered some problems with leaking, thought to be due to the vibration of the screw, causing the planking to loosen and resulting in the ship needing a thorough caulking after just six years of service. Normally ships at this time would require a complete overhall every fifteen years. Her days came to an end in 1884 when she was sold to be broken up at Charlton, a short distance from her launch just thirty years earlier.

HMS *Edgar* launched at Woolwich in October 1858. A wooden-built, 91-gun, screw-propelled second-rate ship of the line, the *Edgar* was a new design of warship built for the Royal Navy. Serving the Navy for almost fifty years, there was, however, an incident of muntiny recorded on board during 1860 while stationed at Spithead. Some members of the ship's crew, including Royal Marines, were arrested and sent for court martial on board the *Victory* at Portsmouth, accused of mutinous acts including causing a disturbance and disobeying orders. The *Edgar* ended her days as a customs quarantine ship.

Opposite above: The steam frigate HMS *Bristol* launched at Woolwich in 1861. During the first half of the nineteenth century, steam warships used paddlewheels either side of the hull, but during the 1850s warship designers favoured propellors and sail that made ships more efficient. Frigates operated independently all around the world, so conservation of fuel 'coal' was extremely important. HMS *Bristol* saw service off the west coast of Africa and South America.

Opposite below: HMS *Anson*, launched in Woolwich in 1860, was one of the last wooden-screw battleships to be built at the dockyard. A Revenge-class, second-rate ship of the line, *Anson* had a complement of 860 men and carried 91 guns on two decks. In 1883 she was re-named *Algiers*, and at the end of her life was scrapped for salvage in 1904.

During the latter part of the 1800s, Britain's armed forces, especially the Royal Navy, were active in all parts of the world. British forces were sent to conflicts throughout the globe, including the Crimea, Eygpt, Sudan, China, South Africa and India. This image shows saddles being packed ready for transport from Woolwich Docks to Abyssinia in 1867.

The corvette *Thalia* was the last ship to be built at Woolwich before the dockyard's closure in 1869. Built specifically as a troop carrier, her sister ship *Juno* had been built two years earlier at Deptford Dockyard. *Thalia* remained in service longer than her sister, and was eventually sold off in 1920.

Woolwich Dockyard gates on Woolwich Church Street at the turn of the nineteenth century. The gates lead to the main dockyards and slipways that once saw huge wooden- and iron-clad men-of-war launched into the Thames. The building seen through the arch is the Woolwich Clockhouse, now used as a community centre. A few of the original buildings remain along with the gateway but much of this area, damaged by bombing in the Blitz, has been redeveloped for housing.

Ships unloading at Woolwich during the early part of the 1900s. Both Woolwich Royal Dockyard and the neighbouring Royal Arsenal munitions works needed to bring in supplies and stores to keep both sites operating sometimes twenty-four hours a day, especially through times of conflict. In 1821 the population of Woolwich had been around 17,000; by 1871 the figure had doubled.

One of the few remaining dockyard basins at Woolwich from just before redevelopment during the 1980s. When in use, these basins would have had a huge roof erected over them. After the dockyard ceased building warships and closed down, a majority of the workers were laid off, and with the Royal Arsenal also cutting back on workers the population of Woolwich fell on hard times. A fund was set up to help families start a new life overseas, and many took the opportunity to emigrate to Canada.

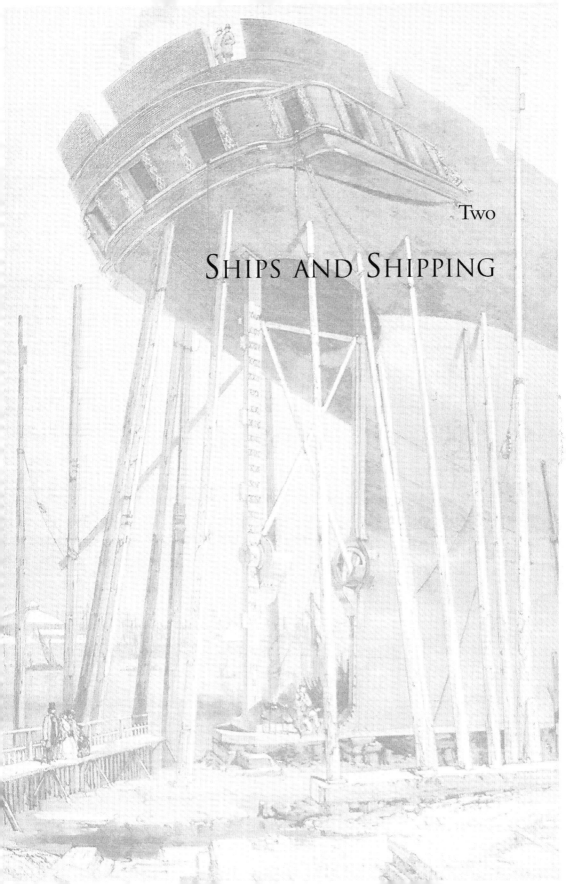

Two

SHIPS AND SHIPPING

In the nineteenth century, a majority of all the world's shipping charts had been using Greenwich as the Prime Meridian for navigation. In 1884 a party of delegates from twenty-five nations voted for Greenwich to become zero longitude, and it was from here that all time around the globe would be measured. Greenwich had truly become 'the centre of the world'.

From ancient times ships from distant lands would have sailed up the Thames to moore off Greenwich – some were raiders, others settlers. In time the area grew in prosperity as royalty built palaces on the foreshore, and commerce and trade evolved along with the Royal Docks of Deptford and Woolwich. With the area expanding through the shipbuilding industry, the south bank between the two dockyards gradually developed into a vibrant waterside community.

Three Woolwich ships, from right to left: the *Great Harry* built in 1512, the *Royal James* built in 1663 and the *Royal George* built in 1755. In the foreground of this period illustration is depicted a vessel of the Ancient Britons to show and re-inforce the ideals of Britain's great maritime heritage. The *Great Harry* was Henry VIII's pride and joy, and at the time was the biggest and most powerful warship in Europe. Although seeing little action, she was used more as a diplomatic weapon, promoting England's power as a nation. It is believed that the ship accidentally caught fire in 1553 while moored at Woolwich, with her remains left to rot on the banks of the river. In June 1667 the *Royal James* was in port at the naval base in Chatham, when the Dutch Navy carried out a raid on the river Medway, which became the greatest Dutch naval victory in history. Several British warships were destroyed or captured, with the *Royal James* attacked and burned by the Dutch fire ships. The *Royal George*, a first-rate ship of the line, saw action in the Seven Years' War during the reign of King George II. Her end came not through war but by accident – while loading stores at Spithead in 1782, the ship took on water through her gun ports and sank with the loss of almost 800 lives, including many women and children who were visiting relatives on the ship at the time. A court of inquiry found the officers and crew free of any blame, as it was decided that the main cause was the general state of decay of the ship's timbers.

Workboats off Woolwich, c.1839. A variety of small vessels, such as cutters, fishing boats and barges, were a common sight on the Thames, and the majority would have been built and operated locally. During the 1500s the development of the shipbuilding industry, especially at Deptford and Woolwich, changed the way large ships and small boats were constructed. Up until this time, seagoing ships were built along the same lines as small boats, and there was no difference between the trade of shipwright or boatwright. All vessels were built in the clinker style, by overlapping planks fastened with nails, but new technology meant ships could be built by laying planks edge to edge in the 'carvel' method, using pre-sawn timbers. These large ships were now built following technical plans, while small boats continued to be built using the older methods.

HMS *Calcutta* off Woolwich in 1846 while taking on stores and supplies at the dockyard. The ship saw action during the Second Chinese Opium War, where the 84-gun, second-rate ship of the line was involved in attacks and raids on Canton. It was also the flagship of Rear-Admiral Michael Seymour, Commander-in-Chief, East Indies and China. Trading in opium was legal during this time, and the British Navy was used to protect British interests in this highly lucrative market.

ILLUSTRATED GREENWICH RAILWAY AND STEAMBOAT COMPANION.

PUBLISHED BY JOSEPH MEAD, RAILWAY OFFICE, 10, GOUGH SQUARE.   [PRICE 3d.

THE OLD ROYAL ROAD TO GREENWICH—
THE RIVER.

Whatever be the course adopted by visitors to Greenwich, they cannot fail to consider that one object possesses surpassing interest : it is the river, the waters of which will often meet the view, though a route by railway should be preferred.

Quaintly, yet forcibly, was it said by old Fuller, " London oweth its greatness, under God's divine providence, to the well-conditioned river of Thames, which doth not (as some tyrant rivers in Europe) abuse its strength in a destructive way, but employeth its greatness in goodness, to be beneficial for commerce by the reciprocation of the tide therein. Hence it was that when King James, offended with the City, threatened he would remove his court to another place, the

Lord Mayor, boldly enough, retorted, that he might remove his court at pleasure, but could not remove the Thames !"

The river has, indeed, been considered for ages the special care and property of the metropolis-city. A jurisdiction is, therefore, claimed by the corporation, extending from seaward, about thirty-seven miles above London-bridge, to a stone on the Essex shore in the estuary—a navigation of upwards of eighty miles. Hence we read and hear of the Lord Mayor, as the conservator of the Thames, in his state barge, attended by his principal officers, proceeding to inspect various parts of the river, a practice which, though it may offer some fun to our contemporary "Punch," confers, doubtless, some advantages on the public.

"NO. 12 WATERMAN."

What a marvellous commercial highway is this! Long before the time of steam-boats and railways, and even high roads and coaches, people went by the Thames from one part of the neighbourhood of London to another. Not only did the humbler orders take "the silent highway," but the nobles prided themselves on the splendour of their barges, the number of their watermen, and the gayness of their liveries. The river was, at the same time, " a royal road," for kings and their families proceeded by the Thames from its banks at Westminster to the Palaces of Windsor or Greenwich.

The removal of the old London-bridge and the erection of the new one is its stead was a work of great importance to the commercial community of London. Owing to the contracted arches, and the great space they occupied, there was a fall of nearly, and sometimes quite, five feet at low water, so that it was dangerous either to ascend or descend the river. The erection of new London-bridge has reduced that fall to two inches instead of five feet, and, consequently, there is a freer access above the bridge ; the bottom of the river is many parts, which before was thick and muddy, is now continually being washed away, and, instead of the water becoming gradually

shallower and fouler, there is a clean gravel bottom, and the channel in many parts is gradually deepening.

Immediately on the eastside of London-bridge is the Adelaide-wharf, and soon the passenger by steam-vessel finds himself opposite the Custom-house. The existence of such an establishment is traced to the end of the fourteenth century. The river front of the present edifice, which cost £640,000, is 488 feet in length. The well-known "long-room," where the public business is despatched, is 186 feet in length, and sixty in width and height. London may truly be styled "the emporium of all the lands of the earth," since the total value of its imports and exports, including the home and foreign markets, is perhaps not overrated when it is stated to be eighty millions sterling. The customs of this immense port will necessarily amount to a large sum, and at the establishment just referred to one half of the amount collected in the whole kingdom is received, exceeding ten millions sterling annually.

The Tower of London, long the chief palace and fortress of the Sovereign of England, has from time immemorial been the depôt of arms and accoutrements. It is encircled by a wide and spacious moat, running round the walls and the river. In the centre is the most ancient and conspicuous portion of the edifice—the citadel or keep—called the White Tower, originally the Tower of London, and occupied as a royal palace. It is a massive quadrangular building, and has a turret at each angle, rising considerably above the roof. The turret at the north-east angle, which is the highest and largest, forms an irregular circle, projecting from the walls, and contains a great staircase, which communicates with the whole building. It was used in the reign of Charles II. as an observatory by Flamstead, the celebrated astronomer royal.

What " a forest of masts " is there in the Lower Pool, awakening diversified thoughts and feelings as to our commercial relations with all parts of the globe ! There may be seen the flags of almost every civilized nation. The clumsy and grotesque though bright and gaudy craft of the Dutchman, the trim-rigged Yankee, the piratical-looking Spanish lugger, the smart Frenchman, the rakish and suspicious Mediterranean trader, the dingy collier, the dashing steamer, the Kentish hoy, and the stately Indiaman, with a host of other vessels of various countries and classes, aid in composing a scene which, for variety and extent, is unequalled in the world.

At Limehouse-reach the Upper Pool is entered, the actual port or harbour known under the name extending only about four miles in length ; but, according to the harbour-regulations, the port of London stretches from London-bridge to Bugsby-hole, just below Black-wall, a distance of nearly six miles and a half.

The eye occasionally catch a glimpse from the river of the docks, so worthy of examination of another time. Their extent is to be traced to acts of piracy, which at the present day seem scarcely credible, but which were perpetrated even so lately as the close of the last century. On the river and at the quays there were thieves of the most consummate audacity. During the day they would mark the barges which they meant to pillage at night. They would cut lighters adrift, and follow them till the tide carried them to some convenient place to make sure of their booty. These marauders went by different names, as "light and heavy horsemen," "coopers," "bumboat-men," "ratcatchers," "scuffle-hunters," "mudlarkers," and "river pirates,"

all of whom subsisted chiefly by the most nefarious practices. Long were depredations thus committed on the river merchants ; and Mr Colquhoun has estimated them at half a million sterling annually. The different articles which plunderers obtained were called by slang terms among themselves—as coffee, peas ; sugar, sand ; and rum, vinegar. In one instance the master of a vessel was asleep below, when a party of these villains were weighing its anchors and cables, but, being awakened by the noise, he went on deck to inquire the cause. But what was the result? The pirates courteously stated what they had done, and, wishing him a very good morning, rowed off with their prize !

Such practices were connived at, there is reason to think, by some of the authorities, and officers connected with the wharfs were found to gain considerable profit from the above they took in this nefarious traffic. In the month of October, 1796, a lighter was robbed of five casks of American ashes, of the value of £50. The contents were carried in bags to the house of an opulent receiver, who sat up two different nights for the purpose. The thieves were remunerated by receiving about a quarter of the value, besides being regaled with a supper and liquor, and the watchman had half-a-crown for his civility in taking no notice of the transaction.

The reconstruction of the different docks greatly contributed to put down this system of fraud, which is now effectually prevented by the vigilance of the river police, who traverse the Thames in all directions at night to prevent robbery.

According to the official account, there belonged to the port of London on the 31st of December, 1842, 2,893 sailing-vessels ; of these 2,354, of the aggregate burden of 677,489 tons, were respectively above 50 tons register, while 629, of the aggregate burden of 20,667 tons, were under 50 tons. They were manned by between thirty and forty thousand seamen. About one-sixth of the whole shipping of the kingdom belongs to the port.

The steam-vessels employed in 1839 were 9,144, having a burden of 505,067, of which 9,000 were Mellsh.

The light steam-boats that ship pass so rapidly have superseded the Margate hoy and a vessel of kindred character and time—the Gravesend smack. How great are the temptations to make use of them for a pleasurable excursion ! You have choice of a number ; the light and swift Waterman, with its fascinating series of numbers, or the larger and more substantial Star, the Ruby, or the Emerald. Expense can be no obstacle. How many have travelled from London

H.M. SHIP BELLONA-GUN, OFF GREENWICH.

A copy of the *Illustrated Greenwich Railway and Steamboat Companion* from the mid-1800s. The publication was distributed in the local area, describing the latest developments in regards to travel and trade. The feature focuses on ships and shipping on the Thames at Greenwich and the Port of London. A passage in the article reads, 'What a forest of masts is there in the Lower Pool, awakening diversified thoughts and feelings as to our commercial relations with all parts of the globe!'

Prison ship HMS *Discovery* at Deptford, *c.*1825. Named after Captain Cook's vessel, she was herself used by Captain George Vancouver between 1791–1795 on voyages of discovery to the Pacific. Spending six years as a prison ship, HMS *Discovery* ended her days at Deptford and Woolwich detaining convicts, some of who would be transported to the places around the globe where this old hulk had once sailed herself.

HMS *Warrior* at Woolwich in 1840 serving as a prison ship. The first Royal Naval ship to bear this name, she was involved in two major sea battles, at Saintes in 1782 and Copenhagen in 1801. Although she was not actively involved in the Battle of Trafalgar, HMS *Warrior* towed home the battered HMS *Victory* carrying the body of Lord Admiral Nelson. In 1857 the ship was broken up at Woolwich.

Above: A veteran of the Battle of Trafalgar, HMS *Dreadnaught* is seen here moored off Greenwich near Deptford Creek during the mid-1800s, one of many former ships of the line to be used as hospital vessels during the nineteenth century. The *Dreadnaught* fought a gallant action at Trafalgar capturing the Spanish ship *San Juan Nepomuceno*. After several years acting as a hospital ship she was towed away downriver to be broken up.

Left: The stern of the *Warrior*, the first iron-clad British warship, on the slips before launch in 1860. Although built across the river at the Thames Iron Works, her boilers and engines were built opposite at Penn & Son's Marine Engine Works on Greenwich Marsh. Penn & Son's were pioneers in marine engine technology and the very first marine steam engine was built at the works in 1825. The company's engines were fitted to many Thames-built ships and boats until closure in 1911.

Captain's cabin on a replica eighteenth-century British frigate the *Grand Turk*. The replica is based on HMS *Blandford*, built at Deptford in 1741. The *Grand Turk* was moored near Lovells Wharf in Greenwich during the summer of 2007 while having some work carried out on her. The interior of the ship is a faithful copy of HMS *Blandford*, and the captain's cabin, positioned at the rear of the gun deck, would have been the only cabin on board ship that would have offered any sort of luxury.

Crew's mess deck on the *Grand Turk*. Food for the crew consisted of oatmeal gruel, cheese, weevil-infested biscuits and preserved meat. Fresh fruit and vegetables were in short supply on long voyages, but sailors were issued with regular tots of rum.

An early nineteenth-century brig, or brigantine, moored off Greenwich Reach. To the right of the image is Deptford Dockyard. Brigs were built in large numbers and used as both merchant and naval ships. They were fast and manoeuvrable, and would carry around 16 guns. Many brigs were built specifically as colliers, transporting coal from the north-east to London.

A view of the Thames from the early 1800s. On the left is the Isle of Dogs and in the distance Greenwich, with the hulk of a Dreadnought moored off Deptford Creek. A variety of small river fishing boats are loading their catches; many of these boats would have been built in small yards on both sides of the Thames.

The *Warspite* at Woolwich, *c.*1877, originally launched as a first-rate ship of the line HMS *Waterloo*. The ship saw action in the Anglo-Japan hostilities between 1863–1864, and later became the Marine Society's training ship at Woolwich. After serving as a training ship for almost forty years, the ship was destroyed by an accidental fire while at Greenhithe.

Woolwich-built HMS *Agamemnon* off Greenwich in the mid-1800s. The British battleship was the first to be built with screw propulsion. During the Crimean War the *Agamemnon* was the flagship of the Navy's Black Sea Fleet, and in 1857 made unsuccessful attempts to lay the first telegraph cable across the Atlantic. The cable itself was made and loaded on board the ship from the telegraph works at Greenwich.

The Woolwich steam packet *Sylph* collides with paddle steamer *Orwell* at Greenwich in December 1844. Several lives were lost during this accident, and there were many such collisions on the river during the early part of the eighteenth century. Ships and river craft were increasing in number on the Thames, and with the steamboat companies seeming to have no concern for other small craft using the river while their own boats travelled from one destination to another at speed, the inevitable accidents would occur, resulting in damage to property, craft and life.

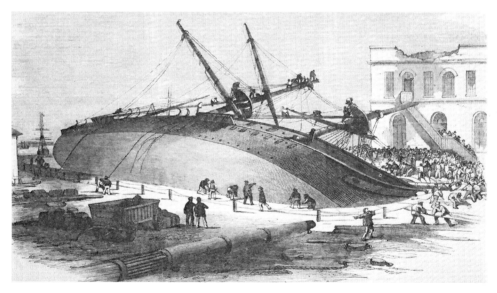

Troopship HMS *Perseverance* turns over in Woolwich Dockyard shortly after having her masts fitted in January 1855. When being floated in the dock ready to be taken out onto the river, the ship rolled from side to side and turned over onto her beam-ends, her foremast crashing into the roof of the chapel opposite. There were around 150 workers on board at the time, but none suffered serious injury. The ship, originally built at Blackwall for the Emperor of Russia but then seized and purchased by the British Government, was repaired and entered the service of the Royal Navy in August 1885.

The barque *Samuel* being raised from the bottom of the Thames near Greenwich in April 1855. Shortly after setting off on route to Jamaica the 500-ton barque went under, and the owners of the three-masted sailing ship would have had to pay the salvage costs incurred for re-floating her. The salvage of sunken ships was nothing new during Victorian times, especially when boats or ships had gone down in shallow waters such as the Thames. There were some quite effective ways to raise lost vessels and cargos during this time – one early invention came by way of placing iron tanks under the wreck and pumping them full of air to bring the vessel up to the surface.

Thames paddle steamer *Metis* is wrecked and beached at Woolwich in September 1867. Ten years previously, the Thames Conservancy Act was passed to control the rivalry between owners of steamboat companies and owners of small vessels trading on the river. In 1909, the Port of London Authority was formed specifically to take over the management of the docks and river.

One of the most tragic events on the Thames occurred at Galleons Reach on 14 September 1878, when the steam collier *Bywell Castle* collided with the paddle steamer *Princess Alice*. The 890-ton collier was returning to Newcastle when she accidentally rammed *Princess Alice*, a wooden-built pleasure steamer packed with hundreds of Londoners returning from an excursion to Gravesend. The steamship smashed through her hull and sent her passengers plunging into the water.

The remains of the *Princess Alice* being salvaged and brought to shore at Woolwich after the disaster in 1878. A majority of the passengers thrown into the water would have drowned, but many died from ingesting the pollutants and sewerage being pumped into the river, for weeks afterwards bodies were still being pulled out of the Thames on both sides of the river. Up until this tragedy there were hardly any rules for how vessels should pass each other on the Thames, as most vessels navigated on the river by way of following the tides and currents. After the board of inquiry rules were established for navigating the Thames, it was recommended that vessels under steam should always pass each other on the port side.

Right: Memorial card from September 1878 for those who died in the sinking of the *Princess Alice.* As the paddle steamer had no passenger manifesto, the exact number that had died was unknown, but it was estimated that around 700 men, women and children perished, and to this day it is the worst loss of life in a single incident on any of the rivers and waterways in Britain.

Below: A fleet of Thames barges moored on the banks of the river near Woolwich, *c.*1905. Such a sight would have been commonplace at one time, when the Thames barge was the most widely used commercial sailing craft on the river. Most barges were built of wood up until the middle of the nineteenth century, and then some were constructed in iron and, later, steel. They were all flat bottomed and had a shallow hull, but all could carry huge cargos comparative to their size. Although used mainly for river and coastal sailing, Thames barges could and did sail to Europe. There are probably less than thirty sailing today, compared to the 8,000 or more sailing during the late 1800s.

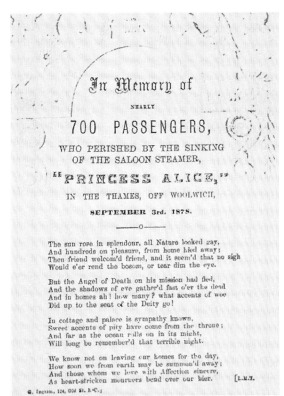

In Memory of

NEARLY

700 PASSENGERS,

WHO PERISHED BY THE SINKING
OF THE SALOON STEAMER,

"PRINCESS ALICE,"

IN THE THAMES, OFF WOOLWICH,

SEPTEMBER 3rd. 1878.

——o——

The sun rose in splendour, all Nature looked gay,
And hundreds on pleasure, from home hied away;
Then friend welcom'd friend, and it seem'd that no sigh
Would e'er rend the bosom, or tear dim the eye.

But the Angel of Death on his mission had fled,
And the shadows of eve gather'd fast o'er the dead
And in homes ah! how many? what accents of woe
Did up to the seat of the Deity go!

In cottage and palace is sympathy known,
Sweet accents of pity have come from the throne;
And far as the ocean rolls on in its might,
Will long be remember'd that terrible night.

We know not on leaving our homes for the day,
How soon we from earth may be summon'd away;
And those whom we love with Affection sincere,
As heart-stricken mourners bend over our bier. [I.M.T.

G. Ingram, 124, Old St. E.C.]

Steam coal colliers off-loading their cargo on the Thames near Woolwich during the early 1900s. Floating derricks could transfer the coal straight into waiting barges, where the coal would be taken to many destinations on the river. A majority of coal brought down from the north-east was needed for industrial use on Greenwich Marsh and the East End of London in the production of gas and electricity.

Royal squadron leaving Woolwich in September 1848 to escort Queen Victoria and Prince Albert to Scotland. Over 5,000 spectators came to watch the royals' departure, and as the Royal Yacht *Victoria & Albert* passed by, a multitude of steamers and riverboats of all types filled the Thames packed full of passengers.

An illustration of the deck of HMS *Foudroyant* after her restoration at Woolwich in 1896. Launched in 1789, the one-time flagship of Admiral Nelson took part in the recapture from the French of both Naples and Malta, and also took several French vessels in the process. The ship was used by the Royal Navy for almost 100 years, and although she was never involved in any major sea battles during her seventeen-year active service, she was extensivley used by numerous admirals of the fleet before taking up a harbour guard role at Plymouth. In 1890 she was sold to George Wheatley Cobb for £20,000.

Middle-gun deck of HMS *Foudroyant*, with a trainee sailor looking over her guns. The ship was to be used by the new owner as an exhibition and training ship for young sailors, to be shown at various fundraising trips at ports and harbours around Britain. After renovations were carried out at Woolwich, the ship, on a voyage to the north-west of England, was wrecked in a storm on Blackpool Sands in November 1897. A salvage of the ship was attempted but failed, and items of wreckage were made into souvenirs and items of furniture.

Royal barges on display at the Maritime Museum Greenwich during the mid-1900s. For centuries the Thames was used for royal and ceremonial events, with royalty travelling on highly decorative barges and shallops. During the reign of Henry VIII the court of the King would often travel by barge up and downriver from his palace at Greenwich to visit the Royal Docks or to attend state occasions. Many of these original barges could be seen on display at the museum.

Three

PASSING TRADE

When the Romans invaded Britain in the first century, they established a trading centre on the Thames, 'Londinium'. Over the next few hundred years, trading ships from all parts of the world sailed to this port that became the capital of England during the Middle Ages.

As the capital and port grew in size, settlements and small villages on the banks of the Thames were gradually swallowed up as the trade and shipping industry expanded along the river. Two-thirds of the country's trade was coming through the Port of London, and local communities were growing in size as vast amounts of working opportunities were generated on the Thames.

As a youngster living in Greenwich, many of my own relatives at that time were working on the Thames, either in industries, factories and wharfs on the river's edge, or working on a variety of ships, boats and barges operating on the Thames.

Large commercial vessels were sailing up and down the Thames using the docks at Rotherhithe and on the Isle of Dogs, transporting and exporting goods of all kinds. Huge ocean liners were docking across the river at the Royal Albert Dock, and the Thames was one of the busiest waterways in the world.

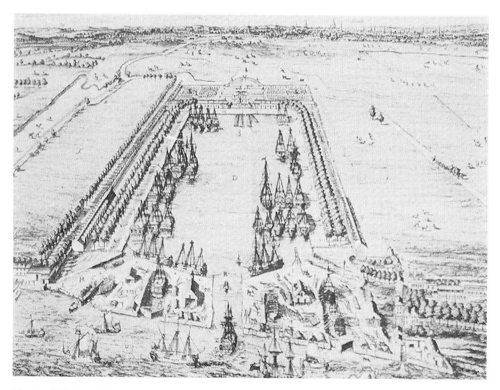

Howland Wet Dock, just west of Deptford Royal Dockyard, during the early 1700s. The dock was built by Wrothesley Russell, who acquired the land from wealthy landowner John Howland after marrying his daughter. The dock was first used by the whaling industry, and in 1806 was sold to a Greenwich timber merchant, William Richie, who formed the Surrey Commercial Dock Company. The docks were expanded during the 1800s to make them the largest enclosed commercial docks south of the river, and at one time huge ocean-going liners used these docks as berths between voyages.

The mouth of the Ravensbourne, a tidal stretch of the river known as the Deptford Creek, which ran into the Thames at Greenwich Reach, shown here in the eighteenth century. Warehouses, factories, wharfages and small ship builders once stood on either bank. There were three corn mills on the river using the tides to drive the mill, with the corn brought upriver by barge. Ships and boats of various shapes and sizes would ply their trade on this stretch of the river, transporting goods to and from this busy little industrial area that divided Deptford and Greenwich.

Coal merchant George Higgs advertising his trade at Crown Coal Wharf on Deptford Creek during the late 1800s, one of the many local businesses on the creek during this time. Coal would have been transported by colliers from the north-east down to the Thames estuary, then upriver for unloading at the wharf.

Extraordinary and Surprising NOVELTY.

May be Seen at Mr. Williams's,

BULL AND BUTCHER, OLD KING STREET,

DEPTFORD,

A FINE YOUNG

FIN WHALE,

WHICH

Was killed off DEPTFORD PIER,

On Sunday last, October the 23rd, 1842,

By a number of Watermen;

It measures about 20 Feet in length, 10 Feet in circumference, and weighs above 2 Tons.

The FIN FISH is as long as a WHALE, but is three times less in bulk. It is known by the fin on the back near the tail, and by its spouting up the water more violently and higher than the whale. The bunch on the head is divided according to its length; that is, at the blowing hole through which it forces up the water. The back is more straight than that of a whale, and the lips are of a brownish colour, appearing like a twisted rope. The whalebone hangs from the upper lip, as it does in the whale; but it does not hang out of the mouth at the sides, as in that animal. The inside of the mouth, between the whalebones, is all over hairy. The colour of this Fish is like that of a Tench; and the shape of the body is long and slender; neither is he so fat as the whale, for which reason he is generally neglected; besides it is much more dangerous to kill one of these than a whale, because his motion is quicker, and he beats more with his tail; so that the people dare not come near him with their boats. The tail is flat like that of a whale, and he seldom appears till the whales are gone.

G, W. Crane, Printer, Flagon Row, Deptford.

A poster from 1842 describing details of a fin whale caught off Deptford Pier in October of that year. This would have been a rare occurrence during Victorian times, and this whale's swim up the Thames came to a grisly end as the men of Deptford dispatched the hapless creature with harpoons and boat gaffs. The whale was put on display for all to see at the Bull & Butcher, Old King Street. During the late 1700s whaling boats sailed out of Howland Dock, close to Deptford, hunting whales in the North Sea. Subsequently, a large whaling industry developed and operated at the docks, processing whale blubber that was used to produce lamp oil.

Opposite below: South Dock, part of the old Surrey Docks, in 2007 is now home to a multitude of private river craft. When Deptford Royal Docks closed down, the Surrey Commercial Docks were still a thriving commercial centre for shipping, but over the years changes within the industry saw the docks fall into decline and they were eventually closed down in the 1970s. The docks have been undergoing a period of redevelopment with most of the docks filled in and residential properties, shopping centres and leisure facilities built in their place.

A Dutch refrigerated cargo vessel, *Wilhelmina-V*, at the mouth of Deptford Creek during the late 1970s. For hundreds of years all types of cargo vessels loaded and off-loaded goods along the estuary dividing Greenwich and Deptford. Industries would have included sawmills, chemical works, coal and timber merchants, breweries, engineering works, gasworks, soap and candle factories and paper mills. Virtually all these local industries have now been replaced by new housing developments.

Boat repair and maintenance yard at South Dock, Deptford *c.2007*. Although there are no longer boats being built on this part of the Thames, some boat repairers are still keeping the old boating traditions going.

The great frost of 1895 at Blackwall, Greenwich. This was the last occasion when the Thames froze, caused by freak weather conditions and a long cold spell. Huge ice flows covered the river, and the disruption to river traffic caused thousands of lightermen and watermen on the river great hardship as they were unable to work. Large steamers were the only craft able to navigate along the Thames, as most other small craft were unable to operate in these conditions.

A Thames sailing barge making ready to moor up alongside Corbett's & Sons, near the Royal Naval College at Greenwich, during the late 1940s. Thames sailing barges had been a common sight on the river for more than 200 years. The barges evolved from a seagoing vessel of the Middle Ages that had a single mast and a large square sail. Although slow, the sailing barge could transport an enormous load compared to how goods had been transported previously – mainly by horse and cart.

A fleet of Thames barges on their way downriver from Greenwich, *c.*1934. Many Thames barges were built and launched at Greenwich Marsh during the 1800s. The last Greenwich Thames barge to be built, *Orinoco*, is still sailing today. The first official Thames sailing barge race was organised by Henry Dodd in 1836, who was characterised by Charles Dickens as Mr Boffin in his novel *Our Mutual Friend*.

The new and the old – barges moored off Greenwich Reach with Thames sailing barges passing by during the early 1900s. Although the Thames sailing barges were still in demand for transporting loads up and downriver, tugs were now towing much larger loads by way of barges without sails.

A tug towing barges off Greenwich, *c.*1934. In the background can be seen lightermen using the flow of the river and a single oar to manoeuvre their barges across the river. Lightermen worked on cargo boats and barges while watermen were licensed to navigate pilot passenger vessels. In 1700 the lightermen petitioned Parliament to join with the watermen, and the Company of Watermen & Lightermen was formed. With a succession of bridges being built over the river, the need for watermen declined, while the lightermen became even busier with more trade on the river.

A pamphlet cover from the late 1800s promoting C. Harding, Italian Warehouseman, War and Tallow Chandler of London Road, now Greenwich High Road. One of the company's products was the selling of tea, which was being imported on clipper ships from China. Horniman's Tea was probably the first tea to be sold in packets and was one of the most famous names in the tea industry during Victorian times. In the early 1800s it could take more than a year for ships to bring back their cargos of tea from the Far East, so faster and more streamlined ships were required – the clipper ship was born. These tall-masted, huge-canvassed ships could travel through the seas at almost 20 knots, drastically reducing the time it took to transport their precious cargo.

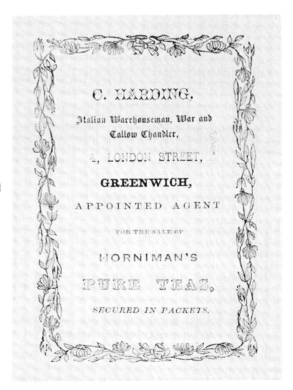

C. HARDING,

Italian Warehouseman, War and Tallow Chandler,

4, LONDON STREET,

GREENWICH,

APPOINTED AGENT

FOR THE SALE OF

HORNIMAN'S

PURE TEAS,

SECURED IN PACKETS.

A painting by the author of the *Cutty Sark*, one of the most famous clipper ships ever to have sailed the oceans of the world. She is depicted sailing through a typhoon on the China Seas off the coast of Formosa, and was painted for a fundraising auction that took place on the ship in May 2003. The clippers would race against time to be the first to return from China and unload their cargo of tea at the docks of London, earning a financial prize for both captain and crew. The elegant clipper ships were a familiar sight on the river, sailing into the Thames Estuary and then towed upriver into the pool of London. Traders in the pool imported tea and coffee from around the world. The City merchants used the new coffee houses as meeting places and Lloyds of London started out life as Edward Lloyds Coffee House near the Tower of London.

The *Cutty Sark* leaving Greenhithe in February 1951 on her way to Surrey Docks. Launched at Dumbarton in 1869, the ship came late to the tea trade, making only eight runs to China before going on to transport wool from Australia. After the ship had spent many years working at sea, she was eventually bought by Captain Wilfred Dowman. On his death in 1938 his widow donated the ship to a naval college at Greenhithe for use as a training ship.

Above: Awaiting restoration and refit, the *Cutty Sark* is moored off Greenwich in June 1952. After a short stay in Surrey Docks while a structural survey was being carried out, she was eventually towed back down the Thames to Greenwich, where this grand old ship remained until the dry dock was ready to take her.

Right: The *Cutty Sark* after being installed in dry dock at Greenwich in 1954. By 1957 the clipper was ready for opening to the public, and was a popular tourist attraction with hundreds of thousands of visitors treading her decks ever since. With a multi-million-pound restoration of the ship underway in 2007, a fire broke out on board which severely damaged this historic ship, but with much of her superstructure, masts and rigging already removed for repair, the damage was not a severe as first feared. She is the only original clipper ship still in existence.

A barge sits on the riverbed off Greenwich Marsh towards the end of the twentieth century. Iron barges were first introduced for cargo carrying as far back as the late 1700s, but were not commonly used until the advent of steam. When steam began to replace sail, the construction of metal barges began in earnest, as powerful steam tugs could now tow more loads in barges than could ever have been transported by a single sailing barge.

Barges owned by W.J.R. Whitehair Ltd moored at Greenwich during the 1970s. The company was just one of many local businesses that operated barges on the Thames, and for more than eighty years barges being towed up and down the river were a common sight, with hundreds moored at wharves and docks all along the Thames. Barges are still seen on the river but are few and far between. As barges increased in size to carry heavier loads the smaller barges were broken up for scrap or left to rust away. An annual barge race takes place from Greenwich to Westminster, where lightermen and their apprentices row these large, heavy vessels with oars, a method once used by lightermen to move a barge from one side of the river to the other.

A barge under repair near Highbridge Wharf during the early 1900s. Barge builders and repairers were commonplace along a stretch of Thames from Deptford to Woolwich, where hundreds of barges were built and repaired by local companies, many of them family-run businesses. The barge builders and repairers were employers of many workers from the Woolwich, Greenwich and Deptford area.

JOHN WADDELL & SONS,

Colliery Owners & Coal Merchants,

GREENWICH WHARF, EAST GREENWICH, S.E.

LOCAL OFFICES—14 ROYAL PARADE and 5 DARTMOUTH ROW BLACK HEATH, 181 BURNT ASH ROAD and 90 HIGH ROAD, LEE.

EVERY KIND OF COAL SCREENED BY HAND. SPECIAL LOW QUOTATIONS TO LARGE CONSUMERS.

PER TON.

BEST WALLSEND	23/-
BEST SECONDS	22/-
BEST SILKSTONE	22/-
WADDELL'S BRIGHT DIAMONDS	21/-
DERBY BEST	21/-
KITCHEN	20/-
COBBLES	18/-
ANTHRACITE STOVE NUTS	24/-
COKE (Broken) per Chaldron, Net	11/-

☞ **1s. PER TON DISCOUNT allowed for Cash**

WITH ORDER, OR ON DELIVERY.

Colliery owners and coal merchants John Waddell & Sons' advertisement from a local publication, c.1897. Coal was the black gold during the Industrial Revolution, and was in high demand for use in factories, industries and the home. There were many merchants on the river dealing in the coal trade who would run colliers to the north-east of England, load up with coal and then transport it back to the capital to be sold for a high profit. Many of these coal merchants became extremely rich in the process, while the miners were paid a pittance for working in hazardous conditions.

Several types of river craft tide up at Ballast Quay in Greenwich during the mid–1900s including Thames barges and coastal steamers. Ballast Quay had been used for over 400 years to load ballast onto ships for their return journeys home. Cargo vessels required ballast after off-loading their goods to make them more stable under sail. The ballast was dug out from pits in Greenwich and Blackheath.

Thames riverbus *Freccia Del Vesuvio* passing the *Cutty Sark* at Greenwich in the early 1970s. Thames Arrow Express ran a hydrofoil riverbus service from Greenwich to central London for commuters as an alternative to train travel. The hydrofoil, fitted at the bow and stern, lifted the boat's hull as the speed increased, enabling the boat to move faster and smoother over the water. Although this was an ideal means of fast transport for commuters on the Thames, the service only lasted a relatively short period of time, and eventually closed down.

The hydrofoil *HS Raketa* (Russian for 'rocket') tied up alongside the pier at Greenwich in the 1970s. This Russian-designed boat was one of several hydrofoils operating on the Thames during this time, running from central London to the Thames estuary. The first hydrofoil service to operate on the Thames was run by Samuel Williams & Sons of Dagenham.

HMS *Ark Royal* moored at Greenwich Reach in June 1987. This was the fifth ship to bear the name; the first *Ark Royal* was built at Deptford in 1587. The original ship was ordered by Sir Walter Raleigh and named *Ark Raleigh*, Elizabeth I bought the ship and re-named her *Ark Royal*. The ship served as the flagship of the English fleet during the attack on the Spanish Armada.

Fireboat *Swift* on the Thames at Greenwich during the 1970s. The London Fire Brigade launched their first self-powered fire boat, named *Alpha II*, in 1900, and have been operating fire-fighting vessels on the Thames ever since. With many warehouses and wharfs standing virtually on the river's edge, any fires in these buildings would be difficult to control from fire appliances attending by road. Fireboats were stationed on the Thames ready to be called into action, and were in constant use during the war years when London suffered severe bombing during the Blitz. Fireboats of today are used for many incidents on the river besides fighting fires, from rescuing people in the water to attending collisions between vessels.

Falklands veteran HMS *Invincible* at Greenwich in July 2005, a month before decomissioning. Her six-day visit to Greenwich followed her return from the Middle East, and the ship played a major part in Trafalgar bicentenary celebrations. The *Invincible* was the sixth Royal Navy ship of that name, and after laid up in reserve at Portsmouth, was eventually sold for breaking up.

The Royal Barge *Jubilant* arrives at Greenwich on 14 September 2002 after her launch during the Queen's Golden Jubilee. The river pageant, a celebration of time, left Isleworth rowed by a crew of Royal Watermen with *Jubilant* carrying Time, a Caesium Atomic Clock, for delivery to the Royal Observatory. The *Jubilant* is a replica of an eighteenth-century oared barge, known as a shallop, belonging to the National Maritime Museum.

Royal Yacht *Britannia* makes her way upriver at Greenwich in November 1997. The Royal Yacht was making her last visit to the Thames as she was due for decommisioning at Portsmouth a month later. Built and launched at Clydebank in April 1953, a year after Queen Elizabeth II's succession to the throne, she sailed over one million nautical miles, docking at 600 ports in 135 countries, carrying the Queen and other members of the Royal Family on official visits. After her decommision, *Britannia* became a visitor attraction at Leith, Edinburgh.

Replica of Captain Cook's ship HMS *Endeavour* at Greenwich during Easter 1997 while on tour around the world. The replica ship was built in Australia using the original plans held at the National Maritime Museum. Captain Cook was the first to determine accurately longitude at sea while on the *Endeavour* using the latest nautical tables and lunar sights. While exploring the southern hemisphere Cook tested a sea clock designed by John Harrison that would enable navigators to fix their position at sea accurately. Many of Harrison's timepieces are on display at the Royal Observatory in Greenwich.

The five-masted sailing ship *Royal Clipper*, the biggest and fastest fully rigged sailing ship in the world, visits Greenwich in July 2000. One of a fleet of sailing ships offering sailing cruises around the world, the *Royal Clipper* has forty-two sails, with a sail area of 56,000sq. ft.

Luxury cruise liner the *World* moored at Greenwich before leaving for Lisbon in April 2002. The ship, a concept of cruise-ship magnate Knut U. Kloster Jr, was built specifically for use by the super-rich as a luxury travelling holiday resort and floating residency for long-term occupation. The ship is over 600ft long, almost 100ft wide, has twelve decks and weighs 43,524 tons.

Cable-laying ship *John W. Mackay* moored at Enderby's Wharf, Greenwich in 1984, with the Royal Naval College in the background. The ship was in service for over fifty years laying and repairing transatlantic cables between Ireland and Newfoundland, sometimes staying at sea for up to three months. The cables were loaded onto the ship at the wharf where telegraph cable manufacture had first been carried out, on a site owned by Glass Elliot, later by Telcon and now Alacatel. Cable is no longer made at the site. Although it was proposed to preserve the ship, she was eventually sold for scrap at Sunderland.

The vintage lighteridge tug *Swiftstone* at Wood Wharf, near Greenwich Reach, in September 2007. The diesel-powered tug was built in 1952 and was owned by Cory Waste Management. The tug was predominantly used to tow barges loaded with waste material downriver for disposal. In 2000 a trust was set up to preserve and refurbish the *Swiftstone* and to promote an active interest in the Thames, past, present and future. With rapid redevelopment taking place along the shore of the Thames from Greenwich Marsh to the site of the Royal Dockyard at Deptford, the *Swiftstone* was relocated to Trinity Wharf at Bow Creek.

The Port of London Harbour Masters boat patrolling a Thames devoid of shipping during September 2007. Although commercial shipping on the Thames has reduced dramatically over the last 100 years, The Port of London still handles over 50 million tons of cargo each year. The PLA is the authority overseeing almost 100 miles of the Thames, from Teddington to the Channel, with the Harbour Master launches carrying out twenty-four-hour patrols, escorting large ships and patrolling local river traffic and Thames Barrier closures.

Dame Ellen MacArthur on her 75ft trimaran *B&Q* after passing through the Thames Barrier in February 2005 during a trip to London to celebrate her record-breaking, single-handed round-the-world voyage, taking seventy-one days and fourteen hours. The boat was built and launched in Australia for the sole purpose of setting the new non-stop record.

A collier off-loading coal at Woolwich, c.1828. The owners of northern coalmines transported their wares by sea in cheap-to-build collier brigs. A fleet of these ships transported coal from the Tyne to the Thames, and in earlier times would have to travel in convoy for fear of attack by pirates intent on stealing their precious cargo.

Sun tugs off Woolwich during 1936, operated by W.H.J. Alexander Ltd of Wapping. *Sun V* towed cutters to Dunkirk in 1940 and during the evacuation a destroyer, HMS *Montrose*, collided with the tug and had to be beached, while the sturdy little tug carried on sailing.

Tug services started operating on the Thames during the early 1830s. The first were coal-powered steam tugs using paddles rather than a single screw, and they had a towing distance of around four miles. As tugs gained more power, working opportunities increased – some tugs operating on the Thames even sailed down into the English Channel to offer sailing ships a tow into the port of London.

A stranded whale at North Woolwich, c.1899. The workers from factories nearby, on finding the whale, stoned and beat the creature to death. The few whales that did happen to find their way up the Thames would be killed for their meat and blubber. The Enderby brothers, who owned land just west of Woolwich on Greenwich Marsh, were one of the last whaling companies to operate out of London.

Merchant ship *City of Ely*, accompanied by a Thames river tug, steams upriver off Woolwich during the 1960s. This would have been a very common scene at the time, when the river was full of ships and boats plying their trade, and transporting their cargos to and from ports all over the globe.

Russian submarine *U475* is open to the public at Long Wharf near the Thames Barrier, *c.*1995. This Foxtrot-class vessel was in service for twenty-seven years with the Russian Baltic Fleet until 1994. After being sold off, the boat journeyed to Greenwich from the naval base at Riga under the command of Captain Vitalij Burda. It was intended that the submarine would be open to the public as a tourist attraction, but because of a lack of visitors, due mainly to where the boat had been moored away from the local tourist areas, it was decided to move *U475* to Folkestone in 1998.

The Woolwich free ferry from the early 1920s. There were three ferries built for crossing the Thames: the *Duncan*, *Gordon* and *Hutton*. The paddle steamers carried 1,000 foot passengers and up to twenty vehicles. Two ferries were in use, while one remained in reserve. There had been a ferry at Woolwich from at least the 1300s, which ran between North and South Woolwich. When it became free to cross the river by the bridges located in London, the people of Woolwich demanded a free ferry crossing, and in 1884 the free ferry began operation.

The *John Newman*, built in 1963, is one of three ferries operating a service across the Thames at Woolwich during the late 1900s. The first three paddle steamer ferries were replaced by a second series of boats in 1922, again paddle steamers. Over a period of time the vehicles they carried became bigger and heavier, and new series of ferries were required to take the increase in loads and passengers. Three diesel-powered ferries were ordered and went into service in the early 1960s.

The Woolwich free ferry terminal on the south side of the Thames, shortly after the official opening in 1889. Thousands of people gathered on the opening day to take a free ride on the ferry, and over the weekend almost 25,000 people arrived by train at the north-side terminal to try out the new service.

The modern view of the Thames from Greenwich Reach towards the Isle of Dogs, c.2007. A fast river bus passes the luxury apartments overlooking the Thames where warehouses and wharfages once stood. In the background is Canary Wharf, a development of high-rise office blocks erected on the site of the West India Docks. Apart from some buildings at the West India Quay, all the original warehouses on the Isle of Dogs have now been demolished.

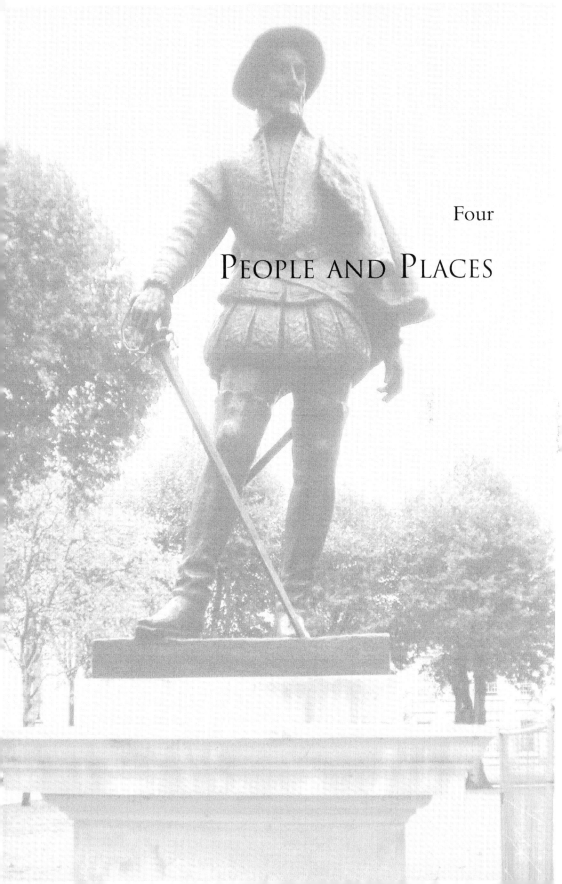

Four

PEOPLE AND PLACES

When the Royal Dockyards at Deptford and Woolwich first started building ships in the sixteenth century, the south bank of the Thames had no more than a few fishing villages on its banks stretching between the two. The Palace of Placentia, the principal residence of Henry VIII, would have been the only major building on this part of the river. With the docks came employment, and soon the villages on the south bank of the Thames expanded into thriving communities.

People not only found work in the dockyards but in the many businesses and industries that grew up alongside the shipbuilding yards. Tradesmen and merchants took advantage of the opportunities coming their way through an increase in river traffic, and soon warehouses and wharfages were being established all along the river frontage. Deptford, Greenwich and Woolwich grew in size to accommodate this expansion of trade and industry, and soon these small villages developed into one of the most prosperous maritime areas on the south bank of the Thames.

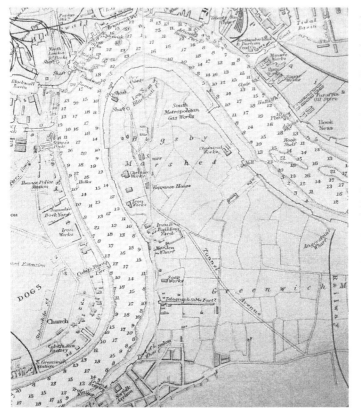

A map of Greenwich Peninsular from the 1890s. A large piece of land to the north-east of the meridian line, Greenwich Marsh had been used for grazing sheep and cattle since the Middle Ages. The majority of the area was owned by charitable organisations, but over the years a small waterside industry developed that included boat-building, barging, fishing and some smuggling. Shipbuilders sited their slips here with the intention of producing some 6,000 boats a year. Clipper ships were built and launched here, and later huge steam engines were fitted into iron warships. By the end of the nineteenth century the whole of the area had been taken over by industrial developments.

Opposite below: Part of Greenwich Marsh after the industries began to close down towards the end of the 1990s. Up until this time ships would have still tied up at many of the jetties and wharfs found all around the marsh, loading or unloading goods and supplies. Almost all of the industrial area has now gone, along with the old buildings used to house them. At the turn of the twenty-first century the whole area was ready for regeneration and the construction of the Millennium Dome.

Glass Elliott during the 1850s. This was the company on Greenwich Marsh developing and manufacturing submarine telegraph cables. Cables from these works were carried by the *Great Eastern*, Brunel's ship built across the river at Millwall, for laying across the Atlantic during 1865.

Blackwall Point on the north of Greenwich Marsh, *c.*1782. In the middle of the image, above the bow of the ship, is Woolwich Dockyard, and to the right of the ship, by the ensign, is a gibbet on the shoreline with some unfortunate swinging in chains. The most notorious of criminal would be hung there to serve as a warning to those intent on taking up river piracy.

View of Greenwich Marsh from Greenwich Park during the 1960s. A majority of the boat-building industry has now gone, replaced by chemical industries, gas works and construction and engineering plants and depots. A small community grew up on the marsh, made up from the employees and their families working and living around the indusries. The workers and their families were accommodated in several rows of terraced housing, and a school, church and several public houses were built in the vicinity.

A stretch of riverfront between the Royal Hospital and Billinsgate Dock, Greenwich, during the seventeenth century. High above the Thames stands the Greenwich Royal Observatory, commissioned by King Charles II specifically for the study of astronomy and for developing a means of fixing longitude as an aid for the navigation of ships. The huddle of buildings on the foreshore were a mixture of wharfs, workshops and private dwellings.

Ballast Quay during the 1960s with the Harbour Master's House to the right of the image. The house, built in 1855, was the control centre of the Harbour Master for directing collier traffic on the Thames. In the background is Lovells Wharf with ships and barges tied alongside, awaiting loading and unloading by a multitude of cranes that once filled this stretch of river.

[This FORM of REQUISITION which is furnished gratuitously to applicants should, when filled, be forwarded, together with the fee, to the SUPERINTENDENT REGISTRAR of the DISTRICT in which the Birth occurred; *not to the Registrar General.*]

SCHEDULE.

THE FACTORY AND WORKSHOP ACT, 1901.

REQUISITION for a CERTIFIED COPY of an ENTRY of BIRTH for the purposes of the above-mentioned Act, or for any purpose connected with the EMPLOYMENT in LABOUR or ELEMENTARY EDUCATION of a Young Person under the age of Sixteen years, or of a Child.

To the Superintendent Registrar or Registrar of Births and Deaths having the custody of the Register in which the Birth of the under-mentioned Young Person or Child is registered.

I, the undersigned, hereby demand, for the purposes above-mentioned, or some or one of them, Certificate of the Birth of the Young Person or Child named in the subjoined Schedule.

Christian Name and Surname of the Young Person or Child of whom a Certificate is required.	Names of the Parents of such Young Person or Child.		Where such Young Person or Child was Born.	In what year such Young Person or Child was Born.
	FATHER.	MOTHER.		
Frank Challis	Henry Challis	Maria Caroline Challis	New Rd Brentford	April 9th 1891

Dated *Thursday* 17 day of *April* 19 0 5

Signature *Henry Challis*

Address *3 Feara St. Greenwich*

Occupation *Boat Builder*

WHEREAS by Section 104 of the Factory and Workshop Act, 1901, it is enacted as follows:— Where the son of any young person under the age of sixteen years, or child, is required to be ascertained or proved for the purpose of this Act, or for any purpose connected with the employment in labour or elementary education of the young person or child, any person shall, on pmaking a written requisition, in such form and containing such particulars as may be from time to time prescribed by the Local Government Board, and on payment of a fee of sixpence, be entitled to obtain a certified copy under the hand of a registrar or superintendent registrar, of the entry in the register, and the Births and Deaths Registration Acts, 1836 to 1901, of the birth of that young person or child; and such form of requisition shall on request be supplied without charge by every superintendent registrar and registrar of births, deaths, and marriages. NOW THEREFORE, We, the Local Government Board, in pursuance of the powers given us by the first section in that behalf, hereby Order as follows:—

ARTICLE I.—The requisition to be made to entitle any person to such a certified copy of an entry of a registry of birth under the section above-cited shall be in the Form set forth in the Schedule to this Order.

ARTICLE II.—This Order shall come into operation on the First day January One thousand nine hundred and two.

GIVEN under the Seal of Office of the Local Government Board, this Twenty-third day of December, in the year One thousand nine hundred and one.

(Sig.) CHAS. T. RITCHIE, *Ex-Officio Member of the Local Government Board.*

(Sig.) H. C. MONRO, *Assistant Secretary.*

A form of requisition from 1905 regarding the employment of Frank Challis, son of Greenwich resident and boat-builder Henry Challis. A factory and workshop Act brought in new legislation to cover health and safety for the employment and education of children. During the early 1900s it was common for children, on leaving school, to become apprentices, following in the trade of their parents. Generations of Deptford, Greenwich and Woolwich residents would have worked in the industries on the river as boat-builders, watermen, lightermen and bargemen.

No. 21...June, 1846.]   [Vol. II.....Price 6d.

JONES's
Woolwich Journal,
AND ARMY AND NAVY GAZETTE.

Published on the First day of every month by E. JONES, at his Library, Woolwich; to whom all Communications are requested to be addressed.

London Agent, MR. H. STARIE, Bookseller, 23, Tichborne Street, Haymarket.

CHARGE FOR ADVERTISEMENTS:—Ten lines and under, 5s.—and 3d. for each additional line.

MATHEMATICAL AND CLASSICAL SCHOOL,
BROOM HALL, SHOOTER'S HILL.

MR. JEFFERY respectfully begs leave to acquaint his friends and supporters that he has removed his Establishment to the above named extensive and commodious premises, which occupy a very elevated, pleasant, and healthy situation, about ten minutes' walk from the Royal Military Academy.

Mr. Jeffery takes the liberty of adding that this change of residence has occasioned no alteration in his system of instruction. In consequence of some of his pupils having recently passed the examination of admittance into the Academy, he has now a few vacancies.

MR. SOLOMON ATKINSON, SENIOR WRANGLER, receives into his Establishment CUMBERLAND HOUSE, Plumstead Common, Woolwich, a limited number of YOUNG GENTLEMEN, preparing for admission into the ROYAL MILITARY ACADEMY, the Military and East India Colleges, and the Universities.

A Prospectus may be had on application to the Principal.

MR. G. CARTERFIELD, who has had much ... experience in preparing pupils on the Woolwich plan, respectfully informs the officers and gentlemen whose sons are intended for Woolwich Sandhurst, &c. ... that he receives a limited number of Pupils to instruct in the departments of Literature and ... subjects to those Establishments.—Terms moderate.

THE WOOLWICH COMPANY'S PACKETS leave Roff's Wharf and Charlton Pier direct for Blackwall, Greenwich, Commercial Dock, Tunnel Pier, London Bridge, Blackfriars' Bridge, Temple Bar, Waterloo Bridge, and Hungerford Market, TEN minutes BEFORE the HOUR and HALF-HOUR, and return from Hungerford Market, Waterloo Bridge, and Temple Pier, at the Hour and Half-hour, Blackfriars' Bridge, Half-past every Hour; and London Bridge Wharf, quarter before and quarter after each Hour.

First Packet from Woolwich, 20 minutes past 8 o'clock.
N.B. Passengers by Boat and Blackwall Railway, First Class 8d. Second Class, 6d.

VOTES FOR THE COUNTY.

FREEHOLD & LEASEHOLD ESTATES, SITUATE IN WOOLWICH AND PLUMSTEAD, KENT.

MR. R. L. DAVIS is favoured with Instructions to SELL BY AUCTION, at his Rooms, WILLIAM STREET, Woolwich, on TUESDAY, the 9th of JUNE, 1846, the following Properties, all of which afford GOOD INVESTMENTS for the Capitalist, and also an excellent opportunity for the enterprising Speculator.

CHARLTON, KENT,
Six and ½ miles from London.

THE RESIDENCE of the LATE MRS. ENDERBY, with Lawn, Carriage drive, Pleasure-grounds, Gardens and Conservatory. The whole in excellent order. The House contains, four principal Bed-rooms, large Drawing-room, two Parlors, light Kitchen, Scullery, Dairy, excellent cellerage, good entrance Hall, and Staircase, Water-closets, &c., a good Coach-house, and Stabling with Servants' rooms over. Held by lease for a term of which about ten years are unexpired. TO BE LET, or the LEASE DISPOSED OF on moderate terms. Fixtures, &c., at Valuation.

For cards to view, and particulars, apply to MR. AUSTIN, Auctioneer and Surveyor, near the Royal Arsenal gates, Woolwich.

Duty off Brandy and Hollands.

T. W. PLAISTED anxious to give his Friends the immediate benefit of the Reduction of duty consequent on the Resolutions passed in the House of Commons, offers his Stock of fine matured COGNAC BRANDY and HOLLANDS at the following prices:—
Martell's Old French Brandy (coloured)....24s. per Gallon
Ditto very old (pale) ....26s.   ,,
Schiedam Hollands ....24s.   ,,
Ditto in Dutch Quarts ....5s. 9d. each.
Family Wine and Spirit Stores,
120, HIGH STREET, WOOLWICH.

A CASE OF PECULIAR AND EXTREME DISTRESS.

The cover of an 1846 edition of the *Woolwich Journal*, featuring an advertisement for steam packet trips on the Thames from Woolwich to London, via Blackwall, Greenwich, Commercial Dock and Tunnel Pier. During the early Victorian period these weekly newspapers and illustrated periodicals became an extremly popular source of information on local and world events.

The *Great Eastern* under construction at Millwall, *c.*1855. After the closure of both Woolwich and Deptford Dockyards, most of the shipbuilding transferred across the river to Millwall and Blackwall. The majority of the large steamships would be built at the Thames Ironworks, Blackwall, including the Royal Navy's HMS *Warrior*.

Captain John Ross, polar explorer and naval officer, departs from Woolwich in May 1829 on his second expedition to find the elusive Northwest Passage. The paddle steamship *Victory* was privately purchased by Ross after the Government refused to fund his expedition. Although Ross never located the Northwest Passage, his expeditions provided an invaluable source of knowledge with regard to the surveys and work he carried out in polar waters, and he was subsequently knighted by William IV in 1834.

Piper's barge-builders dinner, *c.*1933. James Piper built sailing barges at Piper's Wharf on the west side of the Greenwich Peninsular during the late 1800s. Piper's went on to build and repair many other types of river craft at their yard. Many of the early Piper's barges were winners of the competitive barge races that regularly took place on the Thames. Piper's Wharf is now under redevelopment, and boatbuilding on this part of the Thames has come to an end.

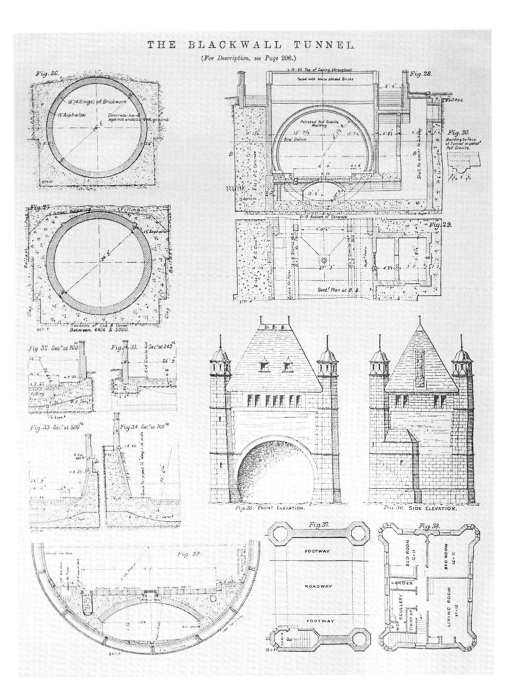

THE BLACKWALL TUNNEL.

(For Description, see Page 206.)

Plans for the Blackwall Tunnel, built at Blackwall Point, *c.*1897. On completion Blackwall Tunnel was the longest underwater tunnel in the world. During the building process many old residential houses had to be demolished on Greenwich Marsh. One was reputedly owned by Sir Walter Raleigh and it was said that this was where a pipe was smoked in England for the first time.

An illustrated view of a stretch of river from the 1800s, with High Bridge Wharf on the left and Deptford Dockyard in the distance to the right. In between would have been barge and tug repairers, marine engineers, a rowing club, and several inns and taverns. Curlew Rowing Club, the oldest on the tideway, had their headquarters here near to the Trafalgar Tavern, located at the end of the row of riverside buildings. In the centre of the image are the buildings of the Royal Naval College, standing proud overlooking the river, and to the right another famous public house, the Ship Inn, is located at a place where the clipper ship *Cutty Sark* is in dry dock today.

Lovells Wharf in the early 1960s. Many wharfs lined the southern shore of the Thames where river boats, coasters and larger seagoing vessels once tied up to load or unload their cargo. The two large cranes, Scotch Derricks, seen on the right of the picture, were thought to have been the last of their kind on the river. Unfortunately, they were dismantled and removed when the site was being cleared for redevelopment.

Lovells Wharf was originally used for handling coal, then later shipments of various metals. The famous old wall, spelling out the wharf name in large white letters, has now been demolished along with many other riverside buildings in the area, ready to be replaced by apartments, workshop studios, a hotel and sports and leisure facilities.

Wooden sail and steamships off Greenwich Reach at the turn of the twentieth century. With both steam and sail-powered craft operating together on the Thames during this period, the area offered employment to the local population in all forms of maritime industry.

Barge breakers at Woolwich during the 1960s. Hundreds of these wooden barges were broken up, to be replaced by steel-built barges towed by tugs. To the left of the picture in the distance is a Thames sailing barge, perhaps on one last trip upriver. Ships, barges and river vessels had been built on the banks of Greenwich Marsh for hundreds of years; one of the last companies to do so were barge-builders Humphrey and Grey.

A ship being caulked during the mid-1800s on the shores of the Isle of Dogs opposite Greenwich Hospital. Ship repairs were carried out on all parts of the river during these times, and the Thames, full of sailing vessles of all shapes and sizes, offered a lucrative trade to shipwrights in the local area.

Enderby's Wharf on Greenwich Marsh during the late 1800s, with the hulk of an old wooden warship, used to store subsea telegraph cable, moored opposite moored. A common sight on the Thames after their seagoing days were over, many were used as hospitals, chapels and prisons for convicts awaiting transportation. Several were used as accommodation, housing around eighty families.

THE PENNY MAGAZINE

OF THE

Society for the Diffusion of Useful Knowledge.

12.]   PUBLISHED EVERY SATURDAY.   [June 9, 1832.

HOLIDAY WALKS.—No. 2.

[Royal Hospital, Greenwich.]

GREENWICH.

The walk to Greenwich is not the most attractive of the walks in the environs of London. It is almost a continued street from each of the bridges; and though the road is wide, and the houses occasionally pretty, the holiday-maker may become impatient for the green fields, and weary of the bustle from which he appears unable to escape. The best mode of visiting Greenwich is by water. For two shillings and sixpence, four persons may take a boat at London Bridge and be landed close to the Royal Hospital; and every day, except Sunday, passage-boats are constantly plying at Tower Stairs, by which passengers are taken for sixpence each. The Thames, covered with the vessels of all nations, may fitly prepare the mind for visiting the palace of those veterans who have sailed under the British flag during many a year of tempest and of battle. Now you will pass alongside the hulk of some immense ship, destined to be broken up, of whose former pride the waterman will tell you some stirring tales, and you may think of these fine lines of Campbell, which stir the heart "as with a trumpet:"—

" Britannia needs no bulwark,
No towers along the steep;
Her march is o'er the mountain waves,
Her home is on the deep."

Again, some steam-vessel from Boulogne, or Hamburgh, or the Rhine, will sweep by, heaving the wave all around in its impetuous course;—and you may reflect how much nobler are the triumphs of peace than those of war, and that the unbounded commerce of England is a better thing for herself and the world than even her proudest victories. In the mean time, the domes and colonnades of Greenwich will rise from the shore, and impress your mind with a magnificence of which the architecture of England presents few examples;—and you will feel an honest pride when you know that few of the great ones of the earth possess palaces to be compared with the splendour of this pile, which the gratitude of our nation has assigned as the retreat of its wounded and worn-out sailors.

When you land, you will not indeed realize the poetical rapture of Dr. Johnson—you will not literally exclaim,

" Struck with the seat which gave Eliza birth,
I kneel and kiss the consecrated earth:"

but you may recollect, with reverence, that Greenwich was a favoured place of this Queen. It was here that Elizabeth might daily behold the real strength of her island empire; and here, as her navy sailed beneath her palace-walls, she might bestow upon her fleets that encouragement which, under the blessing of God, enabled her to effect the destruction of that "*Invincible* Armada," vainly destined, by the ambition of a haughty king, to make England

" Lie at the proud foot of a conqueror."

The greater part of the buildings of the Royal Hospital of Greenwich is stone; the architecture is of the Roman character, rather plain in its general details, but acquiring great features of magnificence from its large dimensions, from the material of which it is executed, from its porticoes, its splendid domes, and its long colonnades. The whole of the buildings are open to the river. On a fine day, the old pensioners may be seen standing about in groups, or taking a solitary walk in

The Penny Magazine from 1832, describing the virtues of taking a trip to Greenwich. By the mid-1800s, Greenwich was a huge tourist attraction for many living in London. With regular riverboat services operating from the centre of the city to Greenwich and beyond, people could travel with ease to gaze on the historic sights on the river and take a stroll around this famous maritime town.

Greenwich Hospital from an etching by E. Walker, c.1852. The buildings were designed by
Sir Christopher Wren, assisted by Nicholas Hawksmoor, and were commissioned by Queen Mary,
wife of King William III, as a naval almshouse for retired or injured seamen. The first occupants arrived
in 1705, and by the early 1800s 3,000 retired or disabled seamen were living there, many of whom had
served at the Battle of Trafalgar.

The Greenwich Hospital naval pensioners from around the late 1700s. The pensioners had their own
uniform and those who were able would earn spending money, around £3 a year, for tobacco and drink
by working within the hospital facilities.

CRICKET!

Surrey Cricket Ground,

KENNINGTON OVAL.

Great Novelty !

On MONDAY, August 30th, and TUESDAY, August 31st, 1852.

Eleven Greenwich Pensioners with

ONE ARM

AGAINST

Eleven Greenwich Pensioners with

ONE LEG.

ONE ARM MEN.	ONE LEG MEN.
Thomas Flavill	Henry Wiltshire
John Graves	Edward Allbar
John Kimberlain	James Allender
Robert Willey	George Jones
John Hill	Wm. Weatherhead
Thomas Cormeck	Thomas Hales
Charles Nash	John Lochlin
Michael Byrne	Wm. Blackburn
James Nimmo	William Croom
James Bedwell	John Rehan
Charles Johnson	Thomas Whitmore

ADMISSION SIXPENCE.

A poster from 1852, anouncing a cricket match played by the Greenwich Hospital pensioners. All the players had either lost an arm or leg during service in the Royal Navy. These old pensioners were great celebrities around Greenwich and would be found in the local inns and taverns recalling times when they were fighting for King and Country.

ANNO DECIMO TERTIO & DECIMO QUARTO

VICTORIÆ REGINÆ.

****

C A P. XXIV.

An Act to enable the Commissioners of *Greenwich* Hospital to improve the said Hospital, and also to enlarge and improve the *Billingsgate Dock*, and widen *Billingsgate Street*, in *Greenwich*; and for other Purposes. [25th *June* 1850.]

WHEREAS it would conduce to the Improvement of the Royal Hospital at *Greenwich*, and the Estate of the said Commissioners of *Greenwich* Hospital in the Vicinity thereof, if a certain Lane or Road known by the Name of *Fisher Lane* in the Town of *Greenwich* aforesaid were stopped up, and if the Soil of the said Lane or Road, and also a certain Dock or Landing Place known as the *Ship Dock* and *Ship Stairs*, on the Banks of the River *Thames* in the Parish of *Greenwich*, which will become unnecessary for the Use of the Public when the Dock known as the *Billingsgate Dock* herein-after mentioned shall have been widened and enlarged, were vested in the said Commissioners, and inclosed within and appropriated to the Use of the said Hospital, discharged from all public and other Rights and Interests in, over, or upon the same, and if the said Commissioners were empowered to purchase and take for the Use of the said Hospital certain Buildings, Ground, and Here-

3 O

ditaments

In 1850, by Royal Decree, an Act was passed to allow the commissioners of Greenwich Hospital to make necessary improvements to the hospital and for the development of areas around Billingsgate Dock on the riverfront. The hospital was a costly business to run, with much of the finances raised through contributions from sailors' wages, parliamentary contributions by way of taxes, naval prize money and even a large sum of money confiscated from the pirate Captain Kid.

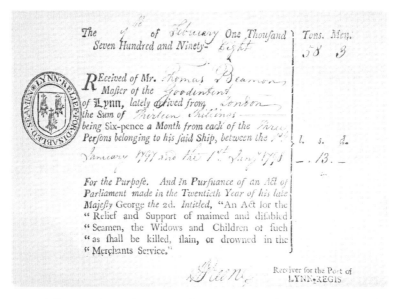

The	9th	of	February	One Thousand	Tons. Men.
Seven Hundred and Ninety-	Eight	58 3

REceived of Mr. *Thomas Beamon*,
Master of the *Goodintent*
of **Lynn**, lately arrived from *London*
the Sum of *Thirteen Shillings*
being Six-pence a Month from each of the *Three*
Persons belonging to his said Ship, between the *1st*
January 1797 and the *1st Jany 1798*

l. s. d.
—. 13. —

For the Purpose. And In Pursuance of an Act of
Parliament made in the Twentieth Year of his late
Majesty George the 2d. Intitled, "An Act for the
"Relief and Support of maimed and disabled
"Seamen, the Widows and Children of such
"as shall be killed, slain, or drowned in the
"Merchants Service."

Receiver for the Port of
LYNN-REGIS

A 1793 bill receipt from a ship's master from Lynn-Regis, for monies paid towards the upkeep and support of injured sailors and their families. The hospital started to purchase property in Greenwich for investment, and later the profit was turned into Government stocks to earn interest. By the late 1800s the number of residents at the hospital had decreased dramatically, and it was decided that it would be prudent to close the establishment down.

The Dreadnaught Seaman's Hospital on Roman Road, Greenwich, during the 1950s. A year after the closure of the residential hospital the vacant infirmary was opened as the new Dreadnaught Hospital in 1870, and named after the hospital hulk once moored at Greenwich Reach. The hospital consisted of several wards and operating theatres over two floors and housed around 250 patients. The hospital treated seamen and also urgent medical cases from the local community.

SEAMEN'S HOSPITAL SOCIETY,
(Late "Dreadnought,")
GREENWICH, S.E.
Dispensary for Out-Patients:—Well Street, London Docks.
(Established on board the "Grampus," 1821. Removed on shore from the "Dreadnought," 1870. Incorporated by Act of Parliament, 1833.)

FREE TO SICK SEAMEN OF ALL NATIONS.
No admission ticket, or letters of recommendation, or voting of any sort required.

SUPPORTED BY VOLUNTARY CONTRIBUTIONS.
Patron: HER MAJESTY THE QUEEN. *Vice-Patron:* H.R.H. THE PRINCE OF WALES, K.G.
President: VICE-ADMIRAL H.R.H. THE DUKE OF EDINBURGH, K.G.
Treasurer: JOHN DEACON, Esq., 20, Birchin Lane, London, E.C.
Secretary: W. T. EVANS, Esq., Seamen's Hospital, Greenwich, S.E.

THE Committee earnestly solicit support on behalf of this universal Charity, than which there is not a more noble or a more useful philanthropic Institution in the world. It gives free relief to all Sailors, without regard to race, nationality, or creed. In confidence of being relieved, sick seamen travel to it from the most distant parts of the kingdom, and find at once a home and a welcome. Safely harboured there, the sailor receives medical aid, skilled nursing, convalescent treatment, and all things necessary to make him speedily able to rejoin his ship and to again maintain himself. There is also reason to hope that the sick seamen become better men by the religious instruction and regular habits which they acquire during their stay in the Hospital.

Since the Hospital was first opened in 1821, upwards of 250,000 sick seamen of all nations have been relieved, from no less than 42 different countries. During 1883 the average number of patients was higher than it ever was before in any one year, having been 8,322 as compared with 5,098, the average of the preceding ten years; while there were more patients in the Hospital than there had been since 1854, the year of the last cholera epidemic.

Under the following exceptional circumstances the Committee URGENTLY APPEAL for additional help. The Sanitary arrangements of the Hospital (built in 1763) are found to be such as are not consistent with the requirements of the present day, and are reported to be in a state that "nothing short of an entire re-construction of the system of drainage will place the Hospital in a safe sanitary condition." In the face of so strong a statement, the Committee feel the heavy responsibility which would be attached to them should any preventible illness break out owing to want of caution on their part, and they have resolved that these alterations should be carried out forthwith. The Admiralty, as landlords, undertake to contribute £1,500 towards the cost, which is, however, estimated to be £7,370, and this leaves £5,870 to be provided by the Committee.

Heavy structural alterations being involved by these drainage works, the Committee avail themselves of the opportunity, long sought, to build a New Chapel. To provide sufficient and proper accommodation in this respect will involve a further cost of £1,281, and consequently the Committee must be prepared with no less a sum than £7,151, in addition to that required for their ordinary annual expenditure.

The Hospital is held under six months' notice from the Admiralty, and consequently the reserve funds are not more than sufficient to build and equip a New Hospital, should it at any time be necessary to do so; the Committee, therefore, are very loth to draw upon their investments, and they earnestly appeal to the public to assist them in their efforts to raise a special Building Fund.

Contributions and new Annual Subscriptions will be thankfully received by the Bankers, Messrs. WILLIAMS, DEACON & CO., 20, Birchin Lane, London, E.C.; or by the Secretary, at the Hospital, Greenwich, S.E., by whom any information desired will be gladly afforded.

FORMS OF BEQUEST.
A.— FORM OF GIFT BY WILL OF LANDS, &c.
I give and devise to the SEAMEN'S HOSPITAL SOCIETY *All that, &c.* [describing the lands, houses, rents, or other property], *for the use of the said Society.*

B.— FORM OF BEQUEST OF MONEY, &c.
I bequeath to the SEAMEN'S HOSPITAL SOCIETY *the sum of £   for the use of the said Society, to be paid free from Legacy Duty; and I declare that the receipt of the Treasurer for the time being of the said Society shall be sufficient discharge for the same.*

N.B.—By a clause in its Act of Parliament (3° GUL. IV., cap. 9) the Society is empowered to receive any Moneys Messuages, Lands, Tenements, Rents, Annuities, &c., whatsoever, not exceeding the value of £10,000 per annum, in addition to any sums of Money to any amount, and any Goods, Ships, &c., of whatever value, which may be given or bequeathed to it from time to time.

[H 24]

A page from a 1950s publication promoting the Seaman's Hospital at Greenwich, and requesting donations and funds to help renovate and carry out much-needed repairs to the building. As shipping on the Thames began to decrease, so did the need for a dedicated hospital for seafarers, and in 1986 the Dreadnaught Seaman's Hospital closed down.

A contemporary illustration of Crane Wharf, depicting a riverfront that had not changed for 100 years or more. R. Moss & Son of Greenwich dealt in scrap iron and rope. To the right is the original Yacht Hotel, in earlier times the Barley Mow, and to the left on the crowded foreshore are several row boats and rivercraft, a common sight up and down the river before the whole riverfront went through a period of regeneration and change.

Corbett's Boat House at the turn of the twentieth century, nestling in between the Yacht public house and the Trafalgar Tavern. The boatyard had a raft floating on the river where small boats of all types were stored. Corbett's, a long-established boat business on the Thames, hired out row boats for business and pleasure. The Curlew Rowing Club had their headquarters at the Crown & Sceptre, seen to the left of the image, and although both buildings have long since gone, rowing is still carried out from here at the Trafalgar Rowing Centre, incorporating both Curlew and Globe Rowing Clubs.

Fishing at Greenwich during the 1700s. There had been a small fishing industry at Greenwich since at least the early 1400s, with fish catches sold in local markets. Fish were in plentiful supply on the Thames before the river became polluted due to the Industrial Revolution. Peter boats were common on the Thames, with many built at boat yards along the foreshore at Greenwich and on Greenwich Marsh. Catches of salmon, roach and shellfish were plentiful and cheap, not only for local people but for inns and restaurants serving up fish dinners.

Parliament ministers at one of Greenwich's famous whitebait dinners during the 1800s. The tradition of holding whitebait dinners started in the nineteenth century during the parliamentary recess on Trinity Sundays. The Liberals favoured the Trafalgar Tavern while the Tories would dine at the Ship, with many MPs arriving by boat from London. Charles Dickens was a regular visitor, dining out with several other literary friends at one of the many hostelries serving up this famous dish.

Fishing for whitebait off Greenwich during the late 1800s. These small silver fish were caught by net and cooked almost immediately. Boats would tie up alongside the Greenwich taverns to sell their fresh catch. Fried up and piled onto plates, the fish would be served with iced champagne, hock or punch.

Billingsgate dock in 1937. The dock, a small inlet off the Thames to the west of Greenwich Pier, is said to have once been the home of Greenwich's deep-sea fishing fleet. It is reputed that a fishing fleet had first sailed and operated from here during the early 1500s. Greenwich fishermen would have sailed out into the Thames Estuary and then up into the North Sea. It is said that, during the nineteenth century, the fleet relocated to the north-east of England and were among the first to invest in the new port of Grimsby. During the war the area suffered from bomb damage, with many of the buildings destroyed and later demolished.

Crowley House during the early 1800s. Originally built in the mid-1600s, the house was purchased by Newcastle iron founder Sir Ambrose Crowley in 1704. Crowley's made ship anchors for the Royal Navy and had warehouses nearby at Anchor Iron Wharf, also known as Crowley Wharf. This splendid Jacobean building was demolished in 1854, along with many other period buildings in the area. The Greenwich power station now stands in its place.

Workers from Robinson's at Anchor Iron Wharf during the turn of the twentieth century. C.A. Robinson, Iron and Metal Merchants, occupied the site once owned by the Crowley Company, and traded in scrap metals. The whole area along this stretch of riverfront was once occupied by many businesses employing local workers from the Greenwich community. The area has now been cleared for regeneration and the construction of luxury riverside apartments.

Above: Greenwich beach at the foot of the Queen's Stairs at the Royal Naval College during the early 1900s. When the tide was low, the local families of Greenwich would often congregate on this small strip of sand and shingle to enjoy some leisure time together on sunny Sunday afternoons, and the children would beach-comb for items washed up on the shore.

Left: Sir Walter Raleigh, the famous sea-farer of Tudor times. The statue, originally on display outside the Ministry of Defence in London, was moved to the grounds of the old Royal Naval College, Greenwich, in 2001. It is reputed that when Queen Elizabeth I visited the Royal Dockyards at Deptford, Sir Walter Raleigh laid down his cloak over a puddle so the Queen could walk over it to save her feet getting wet. A cloak was later included in Sir Walter Raleigh's coat of arms.

An illustration of some of the period houses that once overlooked the river close to Greenwich Pier during the mid-1700s. These rows of weather-boarded houses at Garden Stairs were once commonplace along the riverfront. One of the houses is believed to have been where Dr Samuel Johnson wrote his literary tragedy *Irene*.

OLD HOUSES, GREENWICH

Greenwich steamboat pier in 1850, with a Watermen's Steam Packet Company boat in the foreground full of passengers ready for an Easter Monday trip on the Thames. The pier was built during the 1830s and was later altered to allow the *Cutty Sark* to be placed in dry dock close by. In 1835 the first steamboat service began running trips between Greenwich and London, then downriver to Kent and south Essex.

A lifeboat at Greenwich from around the late 1800s – not such an unusual sight on the Thames during this period of time. This boat seems to have been an historic vessel, as described on a plaque displayed on the boat's bow. Lifeboats of all shapes and sizes were built and launched on the Thames during the nineteenth century; nearly all RNLI boats were built in yards at Limehouse, Shadwell and Blackwall. Surprisingly, the first lifeboats to run a dedicated service on the Thames did not start operating until January 2002.

A recreation of Nelson's funeral procession by barge on the Thames during the bicentenary commemorations, 2005. Admiral Lord Horatio Nelson's body was laid in state in the Painted Hall at Greenwich Hospital after he was fatally wounded at the Battle of Trafalgar in 1805. The streets of Greenwich were crowded by thousands of people coming to pay their respects, before the hero of Trafalgar was taken by barge in a river procession to his final resting place at St Paul's Cathedral.

An illustration of Nelson relics donated to the Royal Hospital, Greenwich in the mid-1800s. Prince Albert purchased the relics for the nation, when the owner, a widow of the Alderman of London, decided to sell them. The bloodstained waistcoat, tunic, breeches and stockings worn by Nelson when fatally wounded on the deck of the *Victory* were on display in the Painted Hall for many years, before being moved to the National Maritime Museum after its opening in 1937.

№ 1 . Royal Barge in which the corpse of Lord Nelson was carried to London.

The Royal Barge that carried the body of Admiral Lord Nelson from Greenwich to St Paul's Cathedral on 8 January 1806. The coffin in which his body lay was made of wood from the mast of the French flagship, *L'Orient*, captured at the Battle of the Nile.

BEHOLD the meed! the splendid honours paid

By grateful England to her Nelson's shade!

At that lov'd name each bosom heaves a sigh,

And drops of sorrow fall from every eye:—

His mighty arm, at one tremendous blow,

Hurl'd Britain's thunder on his country's foe;

But in the midst of his resistless fire,

His conquering fleet beheld their Chief expire!

Though England's ships in awful triumph ride,

With shatter'd navies captive by their side;

The tidings Fame with muffled trumpet brings,

And Victory mourns his loss in sable wings!

Britons! she cries, though now my bosom bleeds,

Your Naval Sons shall emulate his deeds:—

Thus shall his spirit, rising from his grave,

Make future Nelsons triumph on the wave!

Vide "NELSON's TOMB,"—a *Poem, by* WM. THO. FITZGERALD, Esq.

J. G. Barnard, Printer, 21, Snow-Hill.

A poem written for the funeral of Nelson by W.N.T. Fitzgerald, published and sold to commemorate this momentous occasion. Nelson was given a state funeral, normally only reserved for royalty, with thousands crowded along the river to watch the procession pass by.

A model showing the Battle of Trafalgar, made for an exhibition during 1840, and later housed in the National Maritime Museum in Greenwich. The model shows Nelson's ship *Victory* in peril and under attack from the French flagship *Redoubtable*, with the *Tameraire* coming to her aid before eventually forcing the surrender of the French flagship.

A model of a ship of the line on display at the National Maritime Museum, Greenwich during the 1960s. Before redevelopment in 1999, the museum had consisted of galleries, displaying hundreds of ship models from all ages of seafaring, along with some of the greatest marine paintings and a multitude of nautical artefacts that could ever have been seen in one place at one time. The reference library at the museum has the largest collection of historical maritime books in the world, some dating back to the fifteenth century.

London City Council paddle steamer *King Alfred* about to dock at Greenwich Pier for a ceremony during the early 1900s with Thames watermen lining the route for the passengers as they disembark. The pier, built around 1836, was constructed for the use of paddle steamers bringing visitors, tourists, dignitaries or even members of the Royal Household into Greenwich.

Many official visits to Greenwich were carried out by members of royalty for state occasions or festivals at the Royal Naval College, the Royal Observatory and National Maritime Museum since the pier was first built. During the early part of the twenty-first century a new £6 million pier development was completed, ensuring tourists as well as royalty will be able to travel to Greenwich by riverboat for many years to come.

THE Saturday Magazine.

Nº 661.   OCTOBER   22ᴺᴰ, 1842.   { PRICE ONE PENNY.

THE BANKS OF THE THAMES.

THE DOCKYARD AT WOOLWICH.

BLACKWALL—SHOOTER'S HILL—WOOLWICH—PURFLEET.

How great is the difference between the appearance which the Thames presents now, when viewed from Greenwich, and that which it presented twenty years ago! Then, as now, the countless sails, belonging to merchant vessels of all grades, indicated the vast traffic carried on; but we have now the steam-boat traffic in addition thereto. Perhaps there is not now a single moment in the day, from eight o'clock in the morning till dusk, when one or more steamers may not be seen pursuing its swift course either on the western margin of the Isle of Dogs, from Limehouse to Greenwich, or on the eastern margin, from Blackwall to Greenwich. We see exhibited a most extraordinary medley of names—Harlequins and Columbines, Witches, Naiads, Fairies, Nymphs, Diamonds, Rubies, and Pearls, Stars, Satellites, and Vespers, Royal Georges, Royal Williams, Royal Adelaides, in short the ingenuity of steam-boat proprietors seems to have been taxed to the utmost, to find out new and striking appellations for their vessels; and the enormous living burdens which these vessels sometimes carry, sufficiently indicate the favour in which steamboat travelling is now held.

The changes above alluded to are nowhere more conspicuous than at *Blackwall*, especially when taken in conjunction with the introduction of Railway traffic. Whoever was acquainted with Blackwall ten years ago,

knew it as a kind of maritime suburb of the metropolis, where a few ship-builders lived, and also a few maritime men; they knew it as a spot which derived its chief importance from the position which it held with respect to the East and West India Docks; the former bounding it on the east, and the latter on the west. Or perchance they might, as many a wealthy Londoner has done, have gone there to partake of a feast of "whitebait." But now the whole external appearance of the place has changed. If we stand at the gates of the East India Docks and look westward, or at the Brunswick stairs and look eastward, or on the opposite shore of Kent and look northward, we find Blackwall a very much more bustling place than it has ever before been. Let us see in what manner these changes of external appearance have been wrought. Until the recent changes, the premises of a large ship-builder joined those of the East India Dock Company; and both together occupied the greater part of the river frontage at this spot. But the London and Blackwall Railway has been carried in an extraordinary manner, over and under and between and around various parts of these properties, and is brought within a few yards of the river, with a fine quay or wharf between the river and the railway terminus. A handsome and commodious building contains the requisite offices for the railway passengers; while the quay is becoming every year more and more extensively used by steam-boat passengers, who

The *Saturday Magazine* published in October 1842. The image on the cover shows Woolwich Dockyard, and the text gives a colourful description of what it was like on the Thames during the nineteenth century.

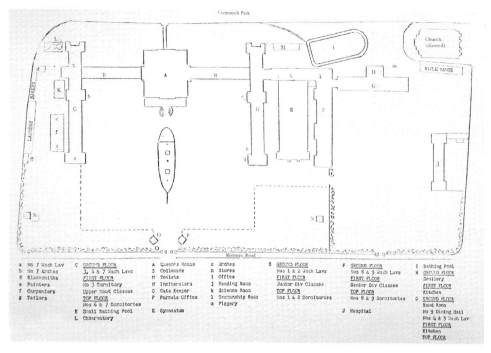

a No 7 Wash Lav	C GROUND FLOOR	A Queen's House	c Arches	D GROUND FLOOR	F GROUND FLOOR	I Bathing Pool
b No 7 Arches	3, 6 & 7 Wash Lavs	3 Collonade	h Stores	Nos 1 & 2 Wash Lavs	Nos 6 & 9 Wash Lavs	H GROUND FLOOR
d Blacksmiths	FIRST FLOOR	M Toilets	i Office	FIRST FLOOR	FIRST FLOOR	Scullery
e Painters	No 3 Dormitory	N Incinerators	j Reading Room	Junior Div Classes	Senior Div Classes	FIRST FLOOR
f Carpenters	Upper Naut Classes	O Gate Keeper	k Science Room	TOP FLOOR	TOP FLOOR	Kitchen
g Tailors	TOP FLOOR	P Parcels Office	l Seamanship Room	Nos 1 & 2 Dormitories	Nos 8 & 9 Dormitories	TOP FLOOR
	Nos 6 & 7 Dormitories		m Piggery			Band Room
	K Small Bathing Pool	E Gymnasium			J Hospital	G GROUND FLOOR
	L Observatory					No 9 Dining Hall
						Nos 4 & 5 Wash Lav
						FIRST FLOOR
						Kitchen
						TOP FLOOR

A plan from 1928 of the Royal Hospital School, now the National Maritime Museum. From the early 1700s a number of boy orphans, including sons of seaman killed in service, were being boarded under the care of the pensioners from Greenwich Hospital. In 1758 a small hospital school was built near to King William Walk to house and educate these orphans. In 1805 the Royal Naval Asylum from Paddington moved to the site, after King George III granted use of the Queen's House at Greenwich for the charity caring for and educating the orphans of seamen.

The Royal Hospital School in the early 1900s showing how much area the hospital eventually covered. Anne of Denmark, the wife of James I, originally commissioned the Queen's House, which was designed by Inigo Jones, and over the years the hospital was enlarged with new wings added for dormitories, classrooms and dining areas. Both schools operated on the site until merging in 1821. Over 800 children were housed at the asylum and in the late 1800s the asylum was re-named the Royal Hospital School.

Training ship *Fame* at the front of the Royal Hospital School during the 1920s. This was the third ship of the same name to reside at the school, all three specifically built as land-locked training vessels that would be manned by a crew of up to 100 young sailors learning the art of seamanship throughout the school year.

On parade at the Royal Hospital School in July 1867 with the boys of the school being presented to Prince George. By the late 1880s the school was caring for over 1,000 youngsters, with most going on to join the Royal Navy. Over 10,000 of these young seamen joined between 1874 and 1930, with five going on to become Admirals.

The dining area at the Royal Hospital School in the early 1900s. Meals at the school were basic and consisted of cocoa and bread at breakfast, with meat, potatoes, pudding and beer for dinner, then bread and milk for supper. Life at the school for these youngsters was hard, entering the school at eleven years old and leaving at fifteen. They would do their own laundry, cleaning and tailoring, as well as learning the trade of seamanship throughout their time at the school. As many of these youngsters came from impoverished backgrounds it was a better way of life than many had previously known.

Boys at the Royal Hospital School ready to start their day during the early 1900s. The day began at six in the morning. After slopping out, washing, dressing and then saying prayers, they would be marched to breakfast for eight o'clock. Afterwards they would be marched to their prospective classrooms. They would have dinner at one o'clock, then an afternoon of more study and exercise before some free time at around five. At six they had supper followed by a period of reading before returning to their dormitories for bed at nine thirty.

A swinging model used during the late 1800s and early 1900s for the instruction of boys on the sailing and handling of small boats. The usual educational subjects were taught at the school, but the majority of the day was taken up with physical activities and learning the skills needed when the youngsters would eventually go to sea, such as navigation, signalling, nautical astronomy and gunnery.

Staff member Mr Bushell, with sailors lining up alongside the *Fame* on their last morning at the Royal Hospital School in March 1923. The school was headed by a Captain-Superintendent of the hospital, and a headmaster in charge of education and teaching. Boys at the school obtained an education for entering naval service at various levels. Some girls were admitted to the school up until 1841, where they were given an education suitable for entering domestic service.

Seamanship room at the Royal Hospital School in 1928, where boys were taught the skills required for entry into the Navy. Although it was still common practice for boys to learn the art of firing cannons and how to repel boarders with pikes and cutlasses, new technology in sea warfare had moved on and the latest advances in navigation and gunnery were an integral part of their education.

Royal Hospital School Band entering the school's main gates during the early 1930s. The boys at the school would carry out many of their drills and exercises to the beat of a drum. On the parade ground, in front of the hospital buildings, the boys would often carry out marching in review order headed by the band, with their colours flying.

On the parade ground in 1927 were some of the last boys to pass through the Royal Hospital School. By the early 1930s the school was oversubscribed by applicants wanting to join the establishment, and in 1933 the school was transferred to a larger site at Holbrook in Suffolk.

The menu cover from the Royal Hospital School Old Boys' Association annual dinner, held on 27 July 1927. The association, founded in 1925 by former pupils of the Greenwich Royal Hospital School, aimed to keep its members in touch with each other and members of staff from the school. Many of those joining the Royal Navy or Royal Marines who had come through the Royal Hospital School were given the nickname of 'The Cradle of the Navy'.

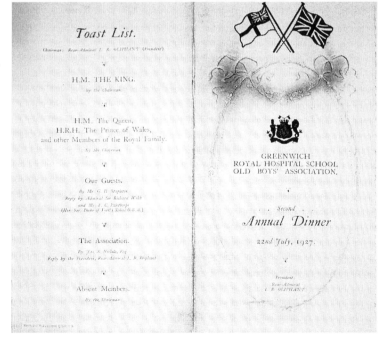

The old Royal Hospital School and the Royal Naval College around the turn of the nineteenth century. Before the Royal Hospital School moved away from Greenwich in 1933, the Royal Naval College had taken over the pensioners' hospital buildings in 1873. The college combined the former Naval College at Portsmouth and the School of Naval Architecture and Marine Engineering from South Kensington.

Royal Naval College staff and personnel line up for a group photograph towards the end of the nineteenth century. Naval officers from all parts of the world came here to train in naval sciences and to study the administrative and staffing policies of their profession.

Two young naval officers at the college during the 1940s. Throughout the Second World War only officers were trained at the college, and over 27,000 naval officers, including 8,000 WRNS, were trained at Greenwich.

Naval officers at the Royal Naval College during the early 1950s. The college consisted of classrooms, lecture theatres and residential accommodation. In 1959 the Royal Navy's Nuclear Science and Technology Department moved in along with Jason, a nuclear reactor that was installed in the King William Building. The Royal Navy left the college in 1998 and the buildings are now occupied by the University of Greenwich and Trinity School of Music.

Left: A cannon bollard at the end of St Alfege Passage, off Greenwich Church Street, *c.*2000. At one time you would have found hundreds of these bollards at the ends of lanes or passageways in Greenwich, Deptford and Woolwich. The bollards were made from cannons off the ships that were broken up and scrapped. A cannon ball would be fixed in the end, and the cannon erected upright in the ground as a means of stopping traffic using the narrow thoroughfare.

Below: Two seafaring vessels of differing sizes that both sailed the seas of the world. In the foreground is Sir Francis Chichester's *Gypsy Moth*, first launched in 1966, and standing proudly behind is the clipper ship *Cutty Sark*, launched in 1869. Both were in dry dock together from 1967 until 2005. Sir Francis Chichester had sailed the *Gypsy Moth* single-handed around the world in 1966, in an attempt to race against the time set by the Australian wool clipper voyages around the world. Queen Elizabeth II knighted Sir Francis Chichester at the Royal Naval College with the same sword used by Elizabeth I to knight Sir Francis Drake a few miles upriver at Deptford. The *Gypsy Moth* was removed from dry dock for a total renovation and subsequent return to the water.

Chicester, the *Gypsy Moth* mooring up on Greenwich Pier to welcome aboard Her Royal Highness Princess Anne. Sailed up the Thames by Dame Ellen MacArthur, Olympic Gold Medallist Shirley Robertson and the daughter-in-law of Sir Francis Chichester, the *Gypsy Moth* moors up near Greenwich Pier to welcome on board Her Royal Highness Princess Anne.

The modern river view from Greenwich Pier in October 2007, devoid of the cranes, warehouses and wharfs that once lined the waterfront, and absent of the ships and barges that were once moored row upon row on the river's edge. A Harbour Master's boat is moored on a jetty next to a service vessel, and the majority of shipping now seen on the Thames comes in the shape of pleasure craft and the odd tug or coastal vessel. Canary Wharf dominates the skyline on the Isle of Dogs, with its high-rise offices and luxury apartments a prominent sight from the river's edge.

Greenwich Reach and the mouth of the River Ravensbourne, known as Deptford Creek, late in 2007. The areas surrounding the creek are now undergoing major regeneration, and luxury apartments, leisure facilities, shops and restaurants will be filling the void left by the demolition of the few remaining industrial properties that once stood overlooking Greenwich Reach. The high apartments on the left of the picture are standing approximately on the edge of what was once Deptford Dockyard.

Remnants of times past: a cannon from a ship of the line positioned at Greenwich Reach, pointing towards the modern apartments across the river. Apart from the major tourist attractions, such as the *Cutty Sark*, the Royal Naval College (now Greenwich University) and the National Maritime Museum, you will find curiosities all along the riverfront, from Deptford to Woolwich, to remind the passer-by of a seafaring heritage long gone.